AS TIME GOES BY

AS TIME GOES BY

REFLECTIONS AND POEMS FOR THE YOUNG AT HEART

MARIE KANE-DUDLEY

CWR

Published 2008 by CWR, Waverley Abbey House, Waverley Lane, Farnham, Surrey GU9 8EP, UK. Registered Charity No. 294387. Registered Limited Company No. 1990308. Reprinted 2010.
Concept development, editing, design and production by CWR
Cover image: CWR from a photo from ImageSource
Printed in China by 1010 Printing International Ltd.
ISBN: 978-1-85345-487-5

This book is dedicated to the memory of
Paul
my beloved son
He was looking forward with eagerness and pride to its
publication, but died suddenly on Christmas Day 2007,
at the age of 42, just one month before its completion.

Also with love and thanks to my children Miriam, John
and Richard, who together with their own families,
and in the midst of our shared grief, supported me with
their love, faith and care so that I was able to pick up
my pen and finish As Time Goes By.

'The LORD gave and the LORD has taken away;
may the name of the LORD be praised.'
(Job 1: 21, NIV)

Acknowledgements

My thanks are due to so many, but first and foremost I give thanks to God who has blessed me with length of days and has enabled me to capture some moments of my long life which I can now share with you, my readers.

To my children Miriam, John and Richard and to their lovely children, I say a huge thank you for allowing me to tell some stories about you! You all taught me so much over the years and I think you're wonderful!

Thank you to my son Richard who steered me towards broadcasting in 1993, and then towards writing this book. You were there to nudge me and then, quite literally, to drive me to appointments with UCB (United Christian Broadcasters) and CWR. You're a great 'enabler'.

Thank you to Michelle Harden, my dear friend – and typist! In this technological age I would have got nowhere without your skills, encouragement, superb reliability and willingness. I am grateful, Michelle!

Thank you to my granddaughter Rachel for checking the grammar. You did it so graciously, Rachel!

Thank you to Mark Stibbe for writing such a moving and generous foreword – I am deeply grateful, Mark.

I am very grateful to CWR for your encouragement and help. Lynette and Sue, you helped me feel at ease in a very foreign field! My thanks also to UCB, as several of my stories I first read in the Word for Today.

Thank you to my dear friend Tessa Feilden, who has agreed to become my personal assistant as the book goes into print.

And finally, to my faithful friends who have supported me with their interest and prayer whilst I've been writing – thank you! I hope you won't be disappointed with the finished article.

Contents

Foreword

I am delighted and honoured to write a few words to commend this remarkable, original and very moving collection of stories. As you are about to see, Marie draws her inspiration from a deep reservoir of personal experiences, some joyful, some painful. She paints in fresh colours and speaks with a unique voice – one that draws you into a world where sometimes you laugh, sometimes you cry.

From a very poor northern UK background, Marie has garnered from life's many challenges a whole harvest of insights. But this is no dry, preachy book, full of dos and don'ts. It is a very rich blending of poetry and narrative, celebrating through singular memories some of life's deepest lessons. Marie has been widowed twice, so she knows the ache of loss and the joys of love.

Many of us live our lives in a state of mental laziness. Life's most precious truths fly past us on the fast-flowing river of our excessive busyness – a busyness for which we were never designed. Only the child, the poet or the contemplative ever pauses long enough to squeeze the juice out of the fruit of observation and recollection. Marie is all three – a Christian poet with a prophetic and childlike wonder for seeing the miracles concealed in the mess of life. Born between two world wars, she has seen many changes and used all of them as a spur to creative and prayerful thought.

This is not a book to speed-read, but rather a landscape of the soul to explore with relish and care. You are about to be invited into the heart of a very thoughtful and resilient woman.

This is what the poet Wordsworth called 'emotion recollected in tranquility'. There are times when it feels as though you're sitting with Marie in a garden, drinking tea, listening to her tell the tales of bygone eras. At other times it feels like you're kneeling with her in a quiet chapel, with warm sunlight pouring through a stained-glass window, listening to Marie pour out her heart in prayer. You are about to overhear the secret history of someone very special, whose character has been refined through suffering and whose life has been made radiant by the Love of all loves.

Enjoy the experience. Cherish the privilege.

Dr Mark Stibbe
Leader of the Father's House Trust
www.fathershousetrust.com

Introduction

Time does indeed go by and, in our later years, we tend to reflect on our memories. I'm sure we all have memorable moments which are easy to recapture.

Many of the thoughts in this book grew from events in my own life, whilst some are from happenings to friends or from things I've read which have impacted me. They are simple stories from which I've learnt important truths. Jesus Himself used everyday things and events to teach us and so I dare to follow His example.

Storytelling has always been part of my life. My ancestors were all from the Emerald Isle so perhaps it's the Irish gene manifesting! Suffice to say, my father used to tell us fairytales when we were small, and I loved to listen.

By the age of eleven I had five younger siblings. Most nights we were all packed off to bed as early as six o'clock – probably for some peace and quiet downstairs! Needless to say, although we were upstairs, sleep was not on the agenda. We played great imaginative games and my sister Agnes tells me that every night she eagerly awaited the next episode in my storytelling sagas – all made up as I went along!

Not surprisingly, I eventually became an infant teacher and my ability to tell a story was well used. Next came marriage and four wonderful children of my own, who were, of course, a captive audience!

All my life I'd been a very religious churchgoer, desperately trying to earn my salvation by my own good deeds. That was a joyless and hard road for, of course, I was always failing. There were more black marks than gold stars on my soul's register!

Then in the 1970s, a totally unexpected thing happened to my husband, Arthur, and me. By a series of what I now see as 'God-incidences' (as opposed to coincidences), we were drawn into the Church's charismatic renewal. For the first time in my life I understood that Jesus had died for me personally, and that salvation could not be earned but is a gift from God, freely given to all who will receive it. We gladly received it, were prayed with, were born again of God's Spirit and our lives were changed forever.

The story I then had to tell was not a fairy story but the most amazingly true and joyful story the world has ever heard. Arthur and I spent the next ten years sharing our good news with many people in the Northeast. After Arthur's death in 1993 I entered the world of broadcasting and for the next fourteen years was a regular contributor on *Morning Thought* programmes, first of all for United Christian Broadcasters (UCB) and then for Radio Solent.

This book has grown from those 'thoughts' and I pray it will be a blessing to those who read it. The prayers at the end of some of the stories are short and simple, but my hope is they will act as a catalyst and that readers will be moved to make their own responses by both listening and talking to the God who loves us all more than we can understand, until the great day comes when we see Him face to face. For time *does* go by, and that day will surely come.

1. *Ours*

The patience and kindness of God amazes me. In the autumn of my life, wonders dawn on me now that I wish I'd seen long ago!

For instance – my childhood was spent in the Northeast of England in a very poor, working-class family. When referring to family members we in the North always used the possessive *our*, saying, 'our dad', 'our mam' and so on. Perhaps it's peculiar to that area, for I've never heard it anywhere else. I'm sure it must have emphasised to us, and to others, our 'belonging-ness', and that is something which every living being needs to feel.

For good or ill, our families gave us our sense of identity. How blessed are those who were nurtured in loving homes; sadly, many are not. But even in the most loving of families we have to admit that, beside the love, we perhaps experienced misunderstandings, disappointments, hurt or other negative things. This is because of our very humanness. However well intentioned, we so often get it wrong.

As a parent I can see the mistakes I made and ruefully wish that I'd done some things differently. Deep down, we all long to belong, to be understood, to be accepted and to be loved for ourselves just as we are, and yet to be nurtured whatever our age, in order to fulfil our potential.

The good news is that we can be!

When the disciples asked Jesus to teach them how to pray, He told them to say, 'Our Father' (Matthew 6:9). In the Aramaic it's 'our *Abba*'; in English – 'our Dad'. Jesus was saying, 'Be intimate with your Dad.' He was also saying, 'And I am your Brother.' Is not this remarkable? I am astonished at the wonder of it.

Of course we go to the Father through Jesus, but once we have taken that step of faith in Jesus' finished work on the cross, we are in the family. We have a heavenly Father who understands us better than we understand ourselves. He accepts us and loves us as we are, but loves us too much to *leave* us as we are. His Holy Spirit dwells in us, and works in us to change us to become like our 'big brother' Jesus. We are members of God's own family. We are the most privileged of people. We *belong*.

I belong

I belong – yes, I belong,
No longer need I wander,
For in my heart I know
That I belong.

He calls me His beloved,
His favour rests upon me,
I turn my faltering steps
And journey home.

No longer am I an orphan,
My heart can sing this song,
What joy it is to know
That I belong.

His name is on my brow,
My home is being prepared,
My Bridegroom is awaiting,
A meal is to be shared.

The betrothal now is sealed
by the Holy Spirit of God.
My Beloved is mine
And I am His own,
I belong!

2. *Those chocolate teddy bears*

It always surprises me when I hear people say that men and women are basically good: just observe toddlers at play fighting over their toys or throwing temper tantrums. Not all is peace and harmony in the nursery!

A friend shared this family anecdote with me: seven-year-old Tom and five-year-old Jack were squabbling over who'd get the first pancake off the griddle. Endeavouring to bring peace into the situation their mother said, 'If Jesus' mother ever made pancakes, I'm sure that Jesus would have said, "Let My brother James have the first one."' Quick as a flash, Tom turned to Jack and said, 'You can be Jesus and I'll be James'!

Are we naturally unselfish and good? I don't think so!

I clearly remember an incident in my own childhood when I was about eight years of age. Just read how this little girl, who always tried to be good, fell from grace! In retrospect, I think perhaps it was the first time I deliberately chose to sin.

My mother was in hospital and the aunt who was caring for us sent me and my younger brother to the doctor's surgery to collect some medicine. We were told to walk there and to get the bus back home, for which we were each given a penny.

Temptation lay in the window of the little shop we had to pass. Unfortunately, we didn't pass it but stood gazing in at the array of sweets, which set our taste buds going. The longer we looked … well, the chocolate teddy bears *were* irresistible and the pennies were burning holes in our pockets!

The plot was hatched. The bus money would buy us each a penny's worth of the forbidden fruits; we'd run home and, if questioned, would say the bus had been late. How smoothly one sin led to another! The purchase was made and we scoffed the teddy bears, but the pleasure was short lived and *how* the guilt weighed on me, particularly as I dared not confess my sin.

Conscience is defined as the sense of right and wrong that governs a person's thoughts and actions. It is a gift from God, setting man apart from animals. Throughout our lives temptation is waiting in the wings, but God's other gift which we all have is free will. As we use our free will we can respond to the voice of our conscience by choosing right or wrong. But oh, how we struggle! How often I feel as the apostle Paul felt when he said, 'I don't understand myself at all, for I really want to do what is right, but I can't. I do what I don't want to do – what I hate' (Romans 7:15).

Thank God for Jesus, for as the hymn says:

Can we find a friend so faithful
Who will all our sorrows share?
Jesus knows our every weakness;
Take it to the Lord in prayer.
(Joseph M. Scriven, 1855)

3. *What makes a home?*

'Houses are made with bricks and mortar,
Homes are made with happy relationships.
Houses are filled with household goods,
Homes are filled with understanding and forgiveness.
Houses are used for people to live in,
Homes are used to train people for life.'

When I was a child I would sometimes be despatched on
an errand to Auntie Lizzie's. I liked going there! Auntie Lizzie
was small in stature and firmly fat. She had a round, rosy face,
brown eyes and short, dark brown hair. I liked her voice with
its clear diction and she always looked clean and tidy. Auntie
Lizzie had been brought up in an orphanage, and cared for
and taught by nuns. Her education completed by the age of
fourteen, she helped in the nursery and became the nursery's
teacher while still very young.

Eventually she married my mother's brother, John. Jobs were
scarce in the North East during the 1930s, and Uncle John
had to endure periods of unemployment. But Auntie Lizzie, a
dressmaker, was often busy at her sewing machine and always
cheerful. Amazing as it now seems, I never left her house
empty-handed – a few flowers from the garden perhaps, or a
cake for tea. It seems that she always found something for me.
Such kindness!

Another lovely memory is the cosiness of her tiny living-
room: the old deep sofa set straight in front of the coal fire, and

the little touches that make a place homely – a vase of flowers, a pretty cushion and a picture or two. I can see her now with a feather duster in her hand flicking over her few pieces of furniture. I believe all this had a big influence on me, as I like to make my own home cosy and welcoming – and I even have a feather duster to flick around!

Today's affluent society is a far cry from the 1930s. Sadly, the right addresses, houses and furnishings are the things that give many people their sense of self-worth. The power of advertising is often alarming, as people are persuaded that constant refurbishing will give them their 'ideal home'.

I had fallen into that trap but I learnt a valuable lesson through a very painful experience many years ago. A business failure compelled us to move into a small, 'two-up, two-down' house with no garden. I was devastated. But amazing things happened when we lived there, for we began to learn true values. It was a time of great blessing. Many people, from millionaires to the poorest in society, came to our little home for prayers and help. Invariably, they often remarked upon its cosiness but, more importantly, upon the peace they could feel there.

Psalm 127, verse 1 says: 'Unless the Lord builds a house, the builders' work is useless. Unless the Lord protects a city, sentries do no good.'

Jesus, come by Your Spirit and be an honoured guest in my home. May it be a place where people sense Your presence and Your peace. Amen.

4. *Seeing clearly*

Brendan was a regular at our weekly prayer group. A shy, quiet man, he did heavy work as a builder's labourer but every Tuesday evening would find him making his way to our meeting.

One week, after a teaching on healing, Brendan asked us to pray with him for the healing of his sight. He suffered from tunnel vision, a condition that greatly narrowed his field of vision. So we laid hands on him and asked Jesus to heal him. I seem to remember that my faith felt wobbly but the truth is that the following week, Brendan came back and asked for more prayer because his sight was improving! We prayed each week for several weeks, the improvement continuing until his sight was fully restored. In his book, *Healing*, Francis McNutt (Ave Maria Press, 1983) describes this as 'soaking prayer'– where God goes deeper and deeper until healing is complete.

Our sight is such a wonderful and precious gift. It's a sad fact of life that we often take things for granted until we are in danger of losing them. This was brought home to me a few years ago when the vision in my left eye had deteriorated. Thoughts of a cataract or glaucoma whirled around in my mind and I went with trepidation to the optician. He tested my sight and was puzzled because there was no change in my eye since my last examination. He then picked up my spectacles and the shameful diagnosis was given … hairspray on the lens! I was covered – not with hairspray, but with confusion, yet at the same time immensely relieved!

To have good vision *is* a wonderful gift, but I believe that spiritual vision is a much greater blessing. I also believe that in our fallen state we all suffer from spiritual tunnel vision.

I was once persuaded by a small grandson to go up onto the top deck of the bus. What an interesting ride I had. It was one that I'd done many times in the car, but from my new vantage point I could see far better the houses and gardens that I'd passed so often.

However, think of God's vantage point – He sees all things at all times. Psalm 139, verse 7, says, 'I can *never* be lost to your Spirit! I can *never* get away from my God.' But as for me – how much more am I fenced in by my prejudices, opinions, lifestyle? Am I willing to push back my tunnel vision and allow God to help me see things from His viewpoint?

In our materialistic culture, our spiritual eyesight can be as effectively clouded as was my lens with the hairspray. How powerfully seducing are the advertising techniques and the so-called entertainments which are being constantly 'sprayed' on to the subconsciousness. In Peter's first letter (1 Peter 5:8) he warns us that our enemy, Satan, prowls around like a roaring lion seeking whom he can devour.

But Jesus says in Revelation, '… get medicine from me to heal your eyes and give you back your sight' (Revelation 3:18).

Jesus, please help me to see people and situations as You see them. Help me to see my own prejudices and by Your grace, overcome them. Amen.

Light is dawning

Here I stand Lord,
Light is dawning,
More and more I see the Truth.
Truth is shining,
Clear and glorious,
Truth is You – the only God.

Open more my bleary eyes, Lord,
Soften more my hardened heart.
Closed-up ears, they need your touch Lord,
Weak and ailing, here I stand.
Let me feel your holy heart beat,
Throbbing deep with love for me.
My heart responds and dares to say
All I do, I do for Thee.

5. *Ambition*

We all have aims and ambitions. Some will be small and relatively unimportant; some will be big and seriously important.

My first ambition was to be the lady behind the counter in our local Co-op. I was six and had been allowed to go there (two blocks away) on an errand. We had a dividend number, 3609, which I had memorised to tell to the lady as I gave her the money for the purchase. I watched her write out the amount I'd paid and our dividend number onto a perforated sheet. She then tore off my cheque and, miracle of miracles, there was a carbon copy underneath! The magic of the carbon paper enchanted me. Oh, to be that lady! Such power!

Two years later and the boundaries extended. I would be sent to the doctor's surgery to collect a bottle of medicine. My ambition changed. I could see myself as the white-coated lady who reigned supreme behind an imposing, partitioned-off area and who dispensed medicines. There was an aura of mystery about it all, which appealed!

Another year or two and I'd decided to be a teacher. I'm sure that was because I had a young pretty teacher who wore beautiful clothes. I could see myself in the role. It's obvious that my motives were not of the highest order – very understandable in a young child but what about when we're adults?

Stephen Covey wrote in *7 Habits of Highly Successful People,* 'It's incredibly easy to work hard at climbing the ladder of success only to discover that it's leaning against the wrong wall … when that happens victories are empty and successes come at the expense of things which are far more valuable. If the ladder isn't leaning against the right wall, every step we take only gets us to the wrong place faster!'

In today's fast moving world where stress-related illnesses are so common, it's important for us to set time apart in order to talk to God about our ambitions and to ask Him to show us His plans for our lives. Whatever our age, it's never too late to move our ladders onto the right walls!

I think it's helpful to reflect on how we spend our time and the motivation behind the actions. We learn important things about ourselves in this little exercise. We may see that we're driven by perfectionism, our need of approval or need of an escape route. As Scripture says, the human heart is very devious (Jeremiah 17:9).

Our highest ambition should be to seek God's will for our lives which is what Jesus always did. Psalm 25 verse 12 says, 'Where is the man who fears the Lord? God will teach him how to choose the best.'

To fear the Lord means to let Him be God in our lives: to reverence and honour Him, putting Him before all others. If we do that, we can be sure that He will lead us and help us to choose well.

Dear Lord, please help me to surrender my will to Yours. I want to fulfil Your ambition for me. Holy Spirit, please help me to be guided by You, day by day. Amen.

6. *Camouflage*

Despite all the mother-in-law jokes, my son-in-law Stuart and I have a very good relationship which is why I was once able to send him a really amusing birthday card!

Picture the scene – the pristine garden of a typical suburban semi. We see a perfect lawn; but the man-of-the-house, looking quite smug, has lifted a corner of the grass and is busily brushing the dead leaves under it like a mat! Unknown to him, he has a captive audience – his irate wife, a neighbour looking over the fence, a dog, a cat and birds in the tree! All eyes are focused on the poor fellow. His sin will soon be uncovered!

I'm reminded of a denim skirt I once had. How ridiculous to love a skirt, but I did! Then one day disaster struck: I splashed some bleach onto the front of this favourite garment. Oh the misery! My beautiful skirt was ruined. Then came a brilliant solution in the form of denim patches. I cut out several flower shapes, placed them strategically on my skirt, ensuring that the bleached area was covered and ironed them on. Now I had a 'new' skirt with a unique designer look. 'I hope no one will be able to tell,' was my next thought. Now, why did that concern me? Sadly, the image I wanted to present was too important to me.

In my early days of ministering to people, I was amazed when a beautifully-dressed lady who arrived in a very smart car opened her heart to us and revealed that it was broken. And I recall the millionaire who shared with us that his personal life was in a mess. From the image they presented one would have assumed that all was well in their lives.

'If people knew what I'm really like they wouldn't like me.' Have you ever thought that about yourself? I certainly have. We're ashamed of those hidden things such as critical thoughts, jealous feelings – different things for each of us.

But there is someone who knows all about us, knows us through and through and still loved us enough to die for us. In fact, it was because of our rubbish that He *did* die for us. I speak of Jesus. How *foolish* to try to hide things from God! In Genesis, after Adam had disobeyed God, we read that, 'that evening they heard the sound of the Lord God walking in the garden; and they hid themselves among the trees. The Lord God called to Adam, "Why are you hiding?" And Adam replied, "I heard you coming and didn't want you to see me naked. So I hid"' (Genesis 3:8–10).

Dear Lord Jesus, by Your Spirit please help me to uncover the things I've kept hidden, even from myself and then to bring them to the cross, receive Your forgiveness and resolve by Your grace to overcome the sin that so easily besets me. Amen.

7. *Bitter or better?*

I was once enjoying a coffee in a city shopping centre when a gentleman asked me if he could seat his mother at my table whilst he went into a nearby shop. I agreed, little realising what a delightful experience I was about to enjoy. This tiny lady was 101! Now, I had never met anyone as old as that so I sat up to take notice. She was such good company with her clear mind, lovely smile and good sense of humour. However, the most striking and unusual thing about her was this: she was full of gratitude for her life, telling me that God had been so good to her. Life being what it is, she must inevitably have had sorrows and hardships to bear, but she had found the key to true peace. She obviously had grown to know and to love God as her Father, so much so that she wanted to talk about Him and tell others of His goodness.

On leaving her with her son, I then walked to my bus stop where I was joined by a young lady of eighty! Well, everything is relative, is it not? But what a contrast to my previous chance encounter. This poor lady looked so miserable, and she proceeded to complain about everything. I tried to change the flow but it couldn't be stopped – she was quite determined to grumble. I heard about the poor bus services, the bad weather, her difficult neighbour, and I'm sure I'd have heard much more but for the arrival of the bus. Yes, *I* could get away but that unhappy lady could not escape from herself.

The Bible says that out of the abundance of the heart the mouth speaks (Matthew 12:34–35). I could only think that her heart was full of bitterness.

My son Richard once made the remark that as people get older they grow bitter or better! A timely warning for his mother, perhaps? Certainly meeting those two ladies gave me a graphic picture of this possibility. We cannot choose whether or not to grow older but we can choose *how* we'll grow older.

In his letter to the Philippians, Paul says, 'stay away from complaining …' (Philippians 2:14).

In the Old Testament we learn that the journey of the Israelites to the promised land should have taken eleven days, but because of their murmuring and grumbling it took forty years!

We can practise cultivating an attitude of gratitude. We have a heavenly Father who loves us, cares for us and delights in blessing us. Psalm 34 begins, 'I will praise the Lord no matter what happens. I will constantly speak of his glories and grace. I will boast of all his kindness to me. Let all who are discouraged take heart' (Psalm 34:1–2).

We can turn to the Psalms for wonderful prayers. Here are two verses from Psalm 100 to set us on this path of thankfulness.

'Go through his open gates with great thanksgiving; enter his courts with praise. Give thanks to him and bless his name. For the Lord is always good. He is always loving and kind, and his faithfulness goes on and on to each succeeding generation' (Psalm 100:4–5). Alleluia!

8. *Disappointment*

When my children were small we had a holiday in the Lake District where we rented a cottage in a beautiful, secluded hollow, near which was a sparkling stream.

An endearing memory I have of that holiday is of my four-year-old son Paul standing in the stream, feet in wellingtons, fishing net in hand, trying to catch not a fish, but a duck! It was his daily challenge – and, of course, his daily disappointment! – for his young mind couldn't comprehend that he was trying to do the impossible.

Then I am reminded of this sad little story a dear friend shared with me. By the age of eight she had been fostered by five different families. Having heard other children talking about the 'tooth fairy', this bright little girl had an idea that she put into action when her first tooth dropped out. Telling no one, she hid the tooth under the carpet and planned to take the expected silver sixpence to her mother as a big surprise. Imagine her disappointment when no sixpence appeared.

So we see that disappointment can start early in life. Surely it's part and parcel of being human? Very often we are disappointed with other human beings. Perhaps it's because we expect or even require more of them than they're able to give at the time. And so we're disappointed. The danger is that we then react from the negative emotion that we're experiencing. Typically feelings at such a time could be of hurt, rejection, annoyance, anger, self-pity or bitterness, to name but a few. I know from my own experience that when I yield to one of these negative emotions it monopolises me and I become a victim to it. The other side of this coin is the sobering thought that *I* must have disappointed many people!

What can I do? What can *you* do? The challenge is to ask ourselves the question, 'What would *Jesus* do?' *No one* has suffered the depth of disappointment that Jesus suffered. We are told in Mark (Mark 14:50), that His closest friends forsook Him and fled at the time when He needed them most. In His humanity, He suffered great loneliness and desertion. And yet, after His crucifixion and resurrection He reinstated these fearful deserters and entrusted them with the task of taking the gospel to every nation. He understood their human frailty and was tender towards them. And He says to us, 'Take my yoke upon you and learn from me, for I am gentle and humble in heart, and you will find rest for your souls' (Matthew 11:29, NIV). We can choose to pray God's blessing on the one who has disappointed us. Is this natural? No! But I think when we act in this way we are taking up our cross daily and following Him. As we respond to His grace, He is changing us.

Help me, Lord, to be willing to humble myself, and to allow You to change me through the disappointments that come in life. Thank You for still loving me despite the many times I have disappointed You, and please help me to forgive those who have disappointed me. Amen.

9. *Encouragement*

Do you sometimes – maybe even often – need to be encouraged? I know I do. A word of encouragement when circumstances are hard can put new heart into us and give us the courage to keep going.

The Bible has a good deal to say about encouragement and describes God as an encourager. In his second letter to the Thessalonians Paul wrote, 'May our Lord Jesus Christ himself and God our Father, who loved us and by his grace gave us eternal encouragement and good hope, encourage your hearts and strengthen you in every good deed and word' (2 Thessalonians 2.16–17, NIV).

I am reminded of a story that demonstrates the power of encouragement. A teacher had a class of pupils who were constantly at each others' throats. One day she gave each one a sheet of paper, instructing them to write down the name of each class member and then, alongside each name, one good quality they saw in that person. Then, taking a sheet of paper for each pupil and writing the pupil's name at the top she listed all the good things that had been noted for that person by his or her peers. Distributing the sheets she noticed how amazed they all were as they read such positive things about themselves.

Fifteen years later one of these boys was killed in Vietnam. The teacher and former classmates attended his funeral, after which they gathered in his family's home. At some point the young man's father said to the teacher, 'Look what I found in

Mark's wallet.' Yes, it was the now worn sheet of paper listing the good things his classmates had written about him all those years before. Some of the others then shyly produced similar sheets from purses and wallets. Their teacher was moved to tears. What *power* we have to discourage or to encourage.

In his first letter to the Thessalonians (1 Thessalonians 5:11), Paul says, 'So encourage each other to build each other up, just as you are already doing.' It's interesting to note that Paul not only urges them to encourage others, but also encourages them by acknowledging that they're *already* in the business of encouraging.

The night before His death Jesus prayed for you and for me. He prayed we would come to know that our heavenly Father loves us as much as He loves Jesus. What wonderful words of encouragement! As we believe it and receive it, our hearts will be strengthened by God, Himself. Every human being is of immeasurable value to God and He gives us the privilege of encouraging them.

Dear Lord, thank You for encouraging me. Please help me to be an encourager and thereby to help and strengthen hearts that are afraid and without hope. Amen.

Invitation

My child, I smile upon you
With eyes of love I smile.
I'm helpless – love compels Me
To offer Love Divine.
My outstretched hand is waiting
To feel your hand in Mine.
Chosen child, please trust Me,
I wait for that small sign –
Your weak hand offered to Me,
My strong hand holding yours,
Together we can sing and dance
Or weep in darkest hours.
For I will never leave you,
Your name is on my heart.
I long for you to know
That we need never be apart.

10. *Slipping on a leaf*

It was a day I'd looked forward to with such expectation. I was going to the Christmas concert of the New English Orchestra in which my son John was playing. The concert was in Bristol and, as I have a friend from schooldays who lives in Bristol, I had arranged to spend the day with her. The climax of the day would be that we'd go to the concert together.

All went according to plan. I met Mary and we talked until our tongues were tired ... so much catching up to do! After a superb meal we set off for the concert hall. I think we were both inwardly glowing. Oh yes, it was pouring with rain but our spirits were high. The concert hall was situated at the bottom of a steep incline. As we walked down it, I was aware of the leaves which covered the path and I was trying to avoid them. I failed! My heel skidded on a leaf and down I went. In a split second everything changed. There was no concert for us that night. Instead, we were taken by ambulance to the nearest hospital.

We sat in Accident and Emergency in a dazed state, hardly able to take in what had happened. The pain in my right wrist told me I'd really injured it. We'd both been so blissfully happy and now everything had changed! I had indeed fractured my wrist.

While waiting to be treated, I had plenty of time to think.

When the various parts of my body are functioning normally, how much I tend to take that for granted!

Life is very fragile and things *can* change in a split second. For me on this occasion it was merely a fractured wrist, but two men there were fighting for their lives – one was the victim of a hit and run driver and the other had been shot in the chest. Do I remember, I thought, to live each day as if it might be my last?

Another lesson was the realisation that I am a very independent person. I found it so hard to be in the position of needing help. It was a humbling experience and I feel quite sure it was one I needed to have. I pray that in the future I will be more understanding of people with disabilities.

And of course, I realised just how loving and kind my family and friends are. It was a strange feeling when the roles were reversed and my adult children became my carers.

'You made all the delicate, inner parts of my body, and knit them together in my mother's womb. Thank you for making me so wonderfully complex! It is amazing to think about. Your workmanship is marvellous – and how well I know it. You were there while I was being formed in utter seclusion! You saw me before I was born and scheduled each day of my life before I began to breathe. Every day was recorded in your Book!' (Psalm 139:13–14).

Lord, help me to be grateful to You for my body which You knitted together in my mother's womb. Help me too, Lord, to remember that You are the giver of life. Amen.

11. *Traditions*

Most families have traditions. I think especially of the ways in which we celebrate special occasions such as Christmas and birthdays. But there can also be our everyday ways of doing things, which are handed down from parents to children, and which are usually happily accepted.

On starting school we move into another phase, which has its own traditions: school assemblies, concerts, prize-giving events, sports days. We never question these things, merely accepting that our school does it this way or that.

Nations, of course, have their own traditions. In our own nation we have such memorable occasions as The Last Night of the Proms, Wimbledon, football finals, the State Opening of Parliament, the Remembrance Day services and Bonfire Night to mention but a few. I imagine that we all have an enthusiasm for at least one of them; it has meaning for us. Without meaning we cannot be enthusiastic.

Traditions can give us a sense of belonging, of security. We receive from the past and pass on to the future. It fascinates me to see the traditions brought into my son Richard's family by his Swedish wife, Maria. One small thing is that their children, Dave, Luke and Hannah, have their birthday cake at breakfast-time! Strange to us but not to them!

The meaning within a tradition is important. I once heard this amusing tale: A newly married couple back from their honeymoon were preparing their first meal, a joint of ham. The husband asked his wife why she had cut off one end. 'I don't know, but my mother always did,' was her reply. When mother was asked the question there came the same reply, 'My mother used to.' But when Grandma was asked, she laughed and said, 'I never had a big enough pan!' True? Perhaps not, but it illustrates the point.

The tradition of going to church can be just that – a *tradition* of going to church. Some people might call it 'practising religion'. We might enjoy the ritual, the music, the sermon, and yet never meet the One who is waiting for us to invite Him into our hearts. Jesus came from heaven to earth for one reason only: to make it possible for us to be reinstated into a relationship with God, not to establish a religion. When ritual leads us into God's presence and our hearts respond to Him in worship, it is fulfilling its purpose. But beware of just *practising* religion!

Jesus says to each one of us, 'Look! I have been standing at the door and I am constantly knocking. If anyone hears me calling him and opens the door, I will come in and fellowship with him and he with me' (Revelation 3:20).

Help me, Lord, to get to the heart of the matter and not to be fascinated by the trimmings. Amen.

12. *Coping with loss*

I have four children and nine grandchildren, so over the years I have received many Mother's Day cards; but the one I will never forget came from my youngest granddaughter, Hannah, when she was only six.

In her childish script Hannah had written, 'I'll love you for ever and ever and when you're dead I'll miss you.' What a unique message! I had to laugh, for her childlike honesty delighted me. Somehow she understood that death, loss and sadness go together and that amazed me.

I remember some of the Queen's words in the wake of the Twin Towers tragedy – 'Grief is the price we pay for love.' Yet, to quote Tennyson, surely it is better to have loved and lost than never to have loved at all? Sickness and death are indeed hard to bear, but we know that they are not God's will for us. They are the direct result of Adam's rebellion against His Creator, yet in His mercy and love, God sent His Son to give us the way to rise above awful grief. The night before His own death Jesus said, 'I have told you these things, so that in me you may have peace. In this world you will have trouble. But take heart! I have overcome the world' (John 16:33, NIV).

I have been widowed twice. Arthur and I were married for almost thirty-six years, and he was the father of our four children. We went through many joys and sorrows as couples do; but the most life-changing event occurred in the 1970s when we both invited Jesus to be our Lord and Saviour. We had been churchgoers all our lives but had never fully understood until then Jesus' words, '... no-one can see the kingdom of God unless he is born again' (John 3:3, NIV). The rest of our lives together were then spent joyfully, helping others to find this New Life.

When Arthur was diagnosed with terminal cancer, I was very afraid. I couldn't imagine life without him. But towards the end I felt that God asked me to entrust Arthur to Him. By His grace I was able to do this, and I experienced God's peace in the midst of great sadness.

Some years later I married John, a widower and a good Christian. Amazed to find such happiness together, we were like a young couple making our new home. It was a romantic affair indeed but many of our hopes and dreams were not fulfilled, for John died just twenty months after our marriage, and for eight of those months he was a very sick man. He wanted to live so much, and fought hard to recover. Again, it was a case of surrendering to the Lord. The day came when – together – we were able to offer ourselves and the whole situation to God, asking Him to take care of both of us. And again there came that peace which the world cannot understand.

I once read that pain is inevitable; misery is optional. We can choose to gather to our hearts the thorns of disappointment, which dig in and hurt, or to gather the flowers of God's grace which comfort and bring peace.

Jesus, when Lazarus died You wept. You weep with me in my sorrows. Please help me to surrender myself and my loved ones to You and to trust You with our lives. Amen.

13. *How is your journey?*

Some years ago, and a few miles into its maiden voyage, a prestigious cruise liner limped back to port with engine troubles. Its passengers had to disembark and were accommodated in a five-star hotel whilst engineers set to work. After a week of hopes being raised and dashed on a daily basis, the voyage was finally cancelled. Disappointed passengers were interviewed by media reporters. One man's comment was particularly pithy: smilingly he said, 'We went nowhere – but we did it in style!' I wonder how many people live their lives like that – going nowhere, but doing it in style?

Unlike our ancestors of even one hundred years ago, we live in an age of travel. I find it quite easy therefore to think of life as a journey; each day bringing us nearer to our eternal destination, and each day offering us new opportunities. There are always new things to learn, to see, to hear, to do, as we walk with our Good Shepherd leading us.

For the greater part of my life most of my travelling was done by car until the day came when I decided to surrender my own personal 'travel capsule'. Only then did I realise that indeed it *was* like a well-insulated capsule, inside which travelled the people of my choice. I was in my own little world.

Joining the ranks of the car-less and becoming a bus and train user opened me up to a new world. I started to develop the skill of chatting and being pleasant to complete strangers. This did not come naturally to me, but I was motivated by the thought that every person who comes into my life, however briefly, is dearly loved by God. And so, before embarking on a long coach or train journey, I now ask God to give me the right travelling companion. The result of that is that I have met some beautiful people, have had some most meaningful conversations, and have even prayed with people as we travelled! Yes, we were travelling geographically but some of us were also travelling spiritually – getting somewhere and *not* nowhere. Our eternal home is with God and Jesus has gone ahead of us to prepare a place for us.

Mother Teresa once said that loneliness is the scourge of Western society. There are many people who are skilled at presenting the stylish image but deep down they are lonely and afraid with no assurance of their destination. We can ask God to give us the right word to speak to those we meet on our journey.

Since His ascension into heaven, Jesus has entrusted to us the work He started here on earth; to look out for the lost and the hurting, to love them with His love and to help them find the Way.

Dear Jesus, please help me to see as You see, to hear as You hear, to speak as You speak and to love with Your love on my journey to heaven. Amen.

14. *Nit-picking*

Once a term, and without warning, she'd arrive on her sit-up-and-beg bicycle and the whisper would go round – 'the nurse is here!' The cheeky ones would say, 'It's Nitty Norah', though such an expression never passed my prim and proper lips! But it was true; she'd come to peer into our hair in search of nits – or worse!

A lifetime later, and recalling the scene, it occurs to me that she'd have been a great subject for a cartoonist with her long, pale, solemn and sharp-featured face. So too would we as we stood in a row nervously awaiting our turn to be subjected to 'The Search'. For the poor unfortunates who received a note from 'the huntress' the shame was terrible! They were sent home and excluded from school until cleansed and pronounced *clean*. I always shook with fear in case such a fate befell *me*. Poor Nitty Norah had an unpleasant but necessary job to do.

A dictionary definition of nit-picking is 'a concern with insignificant details, especially with the intention of finding fault'. Sadly, it can be a very satisfying hobby! We may do it in an effort to justify ourselves, or perhaps to make ourselves seem better than others, but whatever the reason it is an unpleasant trait; and whereas the school nurse had to poke and pry into our hair, *we* do not have to poke and pry into people's lives and motives. In fact, in Luke (Luke 6:41) Jesus says, 'Why quibble about the speck in someone else's eye – his little fault – when a board is in your own?' He doesn't dress it up in fancy language, but is saying straight down the line, 'Search your *own* heart, Marie.'

A story I read tells of two taxidermists who stopped to look at an owl in a window and immediately started to criticise it to bits: 'Its eyes aren't natural, its wings aren't in proportion and its feathers aren't properly arranged.' Satisfied, they started to walk away – at which point the owl turned its head and winked at them! Funny, but thought-provoking, for I know how easily I can fall into the trap of criticising. Jesus says, 'Never criticise or condemn – or it will all come back on you. Go easy on others; then they will do the same for you' (Luke 6:37).

I remind myself that God so loved *the world* that Jesus came to save it. Every single person is equally precious to Him. How dare *I* take on the role of judge! That is *His* prerogative and He relieves me of the responsibility, saying to me, 'Be merciful, just as your Father is merciful' (Luke 6:36, NIV).

Dear Lord, please help me let You search my heart. I need to see my own hidden, sinful habits and attitudes, to repent of them and by Your grace grow new ways of looking at and loving others. Amen.

The problem of 'Me'

The problem of Me is always with me,
There's really no escape.
My puffed-up self-importance
Can cause me to despair.

I see now that the root is pride,
My copybook is blotted.
I know that I am failing
A weak and hopeless sinner.

And then I remember that God
Doesn't think I'm hopeless
Jesus died for me!
Will I decrease that He may increase?

For every small dying in me
Allows Him to take His place.
Simple but hard
For the Me is strong!
A lifetime focused on
The Importance of Being Me.

The amazing mystery is
That I am important, for
God has purchased me –
Purchased me with His blood,
So I am His, no longer my own.

Holy Spirit, show me how to
Let Jesus be Lord of my life
For every small surrender of my will
Allows His character to be formed in me.
Because, yes, He first loved me.

15. *Reaching out in mercy*

The history books recount these facts of General Gordon, the great British soldier and administrator of the nineteeth century who was killed in the Siege of Khartoum (1884–85).

He had declined all offers from the British government of money and titles, accepting only one thing – a gold medal on which was inscribed the record of his thirty-three engagements. It was his most prized possession. After his death the medal could not be found. A search was commenced which led to this amazing discovery – he had sent it to Manchester during a severe famine with instructions that it be melted down and the money made to be used to help the poor. The entry in his diary on the date of its sending read, 'The last earthly thing I had in this world that I valued, I have given to the Lord Jesus Christ.'

Here was a man who knew what it was to be in a position of authority and power but who acknowledged a higher authority – that of Jesus Christ. He believed His Word and he obeyed His Word. He reached out in mercy.

In the book of Lamentations we read, 'Because of the LORD's great love we are not consumed, for his compassions never fail. They are new every morning; great is your faithfulness' (Lamentations 3:22–23, NIV).

As I open my bedroom curtains each morning I see the fast-flowing River Itchen. It reminds me of the truth that God's mercies are new every morning and how grateful I am for that, for it's a sad fact that every day I need His mercy over and over again.

We often read in the Gospels that Jesus was moved with compassion. I need my heart to be changed. A good prompt is WWJD – *What Would Jesus Do?*

When we *risk* being merciful we often receive far more in blessing than we've given. This happened to my granddaughter Rebecca. When she and her boyfriend who is now her husband were in their late teens, they went to work on a Christian mission in Uganda. For the first time in their lives they saw real poverty alongside real joy. They saw children who valued the smallest gift, and on leaving they were given a gift by Humphrey, a 23-year-old who was bringing up three younger siblings. He was too poor to even afford mosquito nets but he gave them a wooden plaque which read, 'A Friend Loves For Ever'. They were humbled, and I believe that the Ugandan experience changed their lives, for God is never outdone in generosity.

Jesus, You ask me to be merciful as Your heavenly Father is merciful. Please help me to have a heart of compassion. Amen.

49

16. *'There's nobody here!'*

I once had a wonderful cleaning lady called Bridie. In those days I was bringing up four children and working as a teacher, so a good cleaning lady was essential both for my house *and* my peace of mind!

Bridie was Irish and was in her seventies. She was physically very strong and hard-working and, whatever the weather, would trudge the mile or so to our home three mornings a week. Incredibly, she always brought a little treat for each of the children so, needless to say, they loved her. I still have a papier-mâché crib set which she gave us one Christmas. It's not worth anything, but I keep it because it reminds me of Bridie's kindness.

However, we did have a problem because Bridie was very deaf and it was difficult trying to hold a conversation with her. Because of that I asked her not to answer the phone. Imagine my dismay when a friend told me that she'd rung my number and a voice said, 'There's nobody here.' We never did solve that one, for 'Mrs Nobody' persisted in answering the phone. *Dear* Bridie!

'There's nobody here!' reminds me of an episode in TV's *Lark Rise to Candleford*, when the feckless Caroline Arless was seen lying in bed with her children clutched to her, hardly daring to breathe as the bailiff was pounding on the door. He knew she was in there but he had to walk away, for her silence was saying 'There's nobody here'.

What is life without communication? It is a most wonderful time when a baby begins to recognise its parents' voices and then to respond to them. As the child grows and its will develops, it can choose to obey or disobey; the former bringing blessing, the latter bringing trouble.

How amazing to realise that it is much the same with God and us, for He is a God who communicates with us and who longs to hear our responses. In Psalm 95, the psalmist longs for people to listen to God and not harden their hearts.

As an infant learns to know its parents' voices, so we must learn to recognise God's voice. For me, it is a most precious thing to be able to spend time each day with God; just Him and me. That is how I have learnt to recognise His voice and to practise responding in obedience. God invites us all to come into this Father–child relationship. His Father-heart is sad when our silence says, 'There's nobody here'.

Lord, please help me to choose to spend time each day alone with You. I long to hear You speak to me – to know You as my tender, loving Father, to obey You and to delight Your heart as I speak to You. Amen.

17. *Can we walk alone?*

When a flock of Canadian geese flies north at the changing of the seasons and one of them becomes sick, wounded or shot down, it never falls to the ground alone. Two others always accompany it, one of them usually being its partner, for geese are extremely loyal and mate for life. The healthy birds care for the ailing one, even throwing themselves between it and any threat. They'll stay with it until it either dies or is well enough to fly again. Even then, they will wait to join another flock of geese. Perhaps we humans can learn something from this?

There's a story I once heard about nine young race contestants, all physically and mentally disabled, assembled at the starting line for the 100-yard dash. At the starting gun they all set out to finish – and, of course, to win.

But one boy stumbled, fell and began to cry. As the others heard him they all slowed down, looked back and then, as one, they went to his aid. One of the girls, who was a child with Down's Syndrome, bent down, kissed him and said, 'This will make it better.' All nine then linked arms and walked together to the finishing line.

Helping others along the way, even if it necessitates our slowing down or giving things up, is actually what we are asked to do if we are followers of Jesus Christ, who gave His all that we might live.

At a time when bad news often hits the headlines, I am

encouraged and humbled when I hear news of the thousands of good Samaritans, the unsung heroes who voluntarily devote much of their lives to helping the wounded, the sick and the deprived, getting alongside them for as long as it takes.

In the Gospel of Matthew (Matthew 25:3–46) Jesus speaks about Judgment Day. Inviting the righteous to come into the kingdom He has prepared for them, He tells them that when He was in need they helped Him. Surprised, they say, 'When did we see you sick or in prison?' Here is His reply in verse 40: 'I tell you the truth, whatever you did for the least of these brothers of mine, you did for me' (NIV).

Dear Jesus, Please help me to see You in everyone and to be willing to help others in their time of need. Amen.

18. *Lessons from an armchair*

How strange to learn lessons from an armchair! This is how it happened. My grandson Sam, who was nine, was coming to spend the day with me. Upon arrival, his first request was, 'Please will you take me into town to buy an armchair?' I was flabbergasted! What a ridiculous idea, I thought. Then he produced a £5 note. 'It's all right,' he assured me, 'they cost £4.99. I've saved up and Mum and Dad said I can have one if you'll take me to the shop.' So to the shop we went and Sam was soon the proud possessor of a shiny, plastic, emerald green *inflatable* armchair.

Back home, and before I realised what was happening, he was trying to inflate it by mouth. 'Stop Sam!' I cried. 'Let's read the instructions!' Of course, they proved to be essential reading, explaining how to inflate the chair and then how to care for it.

Whenever we make a purchase, be it a car or a can opener, if we're wise we'll refer to its accompanying manual and thus avoid damaging it or ourselves and also ensure that we'll make the best use of our new possession.

I believe that the Bible is our 'Maker's handbook' and that if I follow its guidelines I will discover the best way to live the life God has given me. In Paul's second letter to Timothy (2 Timothy 3:16–17), he writes, 'The whole Bible was given to us by inspiration from God and is useful to teach us what is true and to make us realise what is wrong in our lives; it straightens us out and helps us to do what is right. It is God's way of making us well prepared at every point, fully equipped to do good to everyone.' Clearly, Paul trusted in and relied upon *his* Maker's Handbook.

Can you bear with me and go back to the plastic armchair? If you can, you'll see Sam happily settled in the chair and watching a favourite video. Happily settled, that is, until I told him it was time to leave in order to catch his bus home. Then came my second shock. Although he was returning to me the following day he wanted to take his armchair home, and expected to carry it – fully inflated – onto the bus! There followed a frantic five minutes as we worked at reducing it to a manageable size!

That episode caused me to think of the things in my own life which I'd imagined would make me perfectly happy, but which had become burdens; burdens that were not so easy to off-load.

The truth is that nothing on this earth will make us perfectly happy; and only when we reach our heavenly home will we know real happiness. In the meantime we are advised by the writer to the Hebrews to 'throw off everything that hinders and the sin that so easily entangles, and let us run with perseverance the race marked out for us' (Hebrews 12:1).

Lord, may I have the wisdom to use Your written Word to guide me in life and please help me to let go of the things that are encumbrances. Amen.

19. *Jesus doesn't change*

Being born between the two World Wars, I've lived through a lifetime of colossal changes. For instance, when I was five, a ha'penny taken to school gave me a turn on the rocking horse – ten rocks backwards and forwards – while the rest of the class looked on with envy. That was a rare treat as money was very scarce.

At 12 o'clock it was home to Mum and a hot dinner. Our dinner *hour* was actually an hour-and-a-half. What a contrast to today when many teachers find difficulty in snatching a ten-minute break!

Without fear we children could go to the local park, taking jam sandwiches and a bottle of home-made ginger beer for our picnic – and yes, we even took the baby in the pram!

Horse-drawn wagons were used for the delivery of coal and milk. My father made a barrow from an orange box and if a horse obliged us with a 'deposit' in the road we were sent out with the barrow to collect it for the garden!

When I was eight our horizons widened. An uncle gave us a wireless set which ran on batteries. We were entranced! When necessary, my brother and I would carry the batteries to a shop for recharging.

Our doctor's surgery was a place of mystery and for me the most mysterious part was a partitioned-off area with a door and a hatch through which I could see the large glass bottles of various coloured liquids. Mistress of all was a white-coated lady, the dispenser, from whom we received the appropriate bottle of medicine. Cherry cough medicine was our favourite brew!

Going to the pictures cost three pence – a rare treat that took us into a world of fantasy. How I *loved* the plush comfort; the pink wall-lights, the sheer luxury of The Palladium, our local cinema. Standing in the queue was a fearful experience: we dreaded reaching the ticket office only to be told all the tickets had been sold.

We had so little in the way of material things and yet we were content. I look at our world today and am convinced that man's cleverness without godly wisdom is not clever at all. The speed of change is frightening. We seem to be hurtling down a slope and there's no way of stopping. The writer to the Hebrews said, 'Jesus Christ is the same yesterday, today, and forever. So do not be attracted by strange, new ideas' (Hebrews 13:8–9).

Dear Lord, I thank You for the material blessings of the twenty-first century. Please help me not make idols of them. May I have the wisdom to keep You at the centre of my life. I am so thankful, Jesus, that You do not change. I can count on Your faithfulness. Amen.

20. *Damaged goods*

A memory that charms my heart is that of my granddaughter, Anna, when she was only two.

She was staying with her grandpa and me for a holiday, so when we went to the local shops, Anna would accompany us, proudly pushing her little doll's pram, beautifully draped with pretty pillow and covers. I recall meeting some friends one day and naturally we stopped to chat. After greeting Anna, they asked to see her dolly. As they bent down to look under the hood they could scarcely conceal their amazement – and amusement – because, lying in all its splendour, was the most ancient and battered-looking toy cat! The poor thing only had one eye, part of a nose, and was minus some whiskers. Our friends quickly recovered and then asked, 'What's his name?' '*She's* called Thomas,' Anna sweetly replied! Who can fathom the mind of a two-year-old? Although she had pretty dolls, Thomas had first place in her heart. She loved her battered old friend, and she was proud of him.

Many of us have taken hard blows in life. Perhaps we feel quite battered because of illness or disability; or maybe we've been so emotionally damaged that we are unable to receive or to give love. Happenings in life can mark us, damage us and make us feel that we're only fit for the rubbish heap. Indeed, the rubbish heap was all that Anna's cat *was* fit for but Anna didn't think so – she loved him! And that's how our heavenly Father feels about us. That is a wonderful realisation! However damaged or un-beautiful we feel, He loves us and it *is* possible to bloom again.

I realised that soon after the death of my second husband, John. Knowing little about gardening, the few potted plants on the patio were grossly neglected. The day came when I noticed that the Hebe shrub was seriously pot-bound and wilting. It seemed to be gazing at me reproachfully and I felt miserably guilty about it. Could it be rescued? I'd try.

Help came in the persons of my son John and his wife Jane, complete with a large pot and fresh compost. Perhaps the Hebe was sulking, but it wouldn't budge! Different implements were used, but the final strategy resembled a tug-of-war with John holding the pot and Jane and I hanging on to the poor plant. Eventually it was released and we then did all we could to make it happy with re-potting and much watering and feeding. I seriously doubted whether it would survive such an ordeal, but it did and was soon looking beautiful.

As I think of Anna's battered toy cat which she loved so much, it reminds me that God loves each one of us even if we feel like damaged goods. What's more: as my wilting Hebe was revived, I remember that God is able to restore and heal *us*.

Psalm 147 verse 3, says, 'He heals the broken-hearted, binding up their wounds.'

Dear Jesus, please help me to believe that You love me and that I am precious in Your sight. Help me to turn to You, the Divine Healer, and allow You to restore me with Your love. Amen.

21. *Being lost*

Have you ever been lost? I have, and I can still vividly recall the fear I felt.

It happened soon after the death of my husband, Arthur. Although I'd been able to drive for many years, he had done most of the driving and I was quite happy in the role of passenger. His illness and death had propelled me into the driving seat but I took to the wheel reluctantly, very fearful of getting lost or the car breaking down.

It was a dark, wet night, and I was driving home in a part of the country which was new to me, when I realised I was lost. This was, for me, *the* dreaded situation – alone in a car on such a night on a strange and lonely road. There was only One to whom I could turn – my God. The words of Psalm 91 came to me: 'Now you don't need to be afraid of the dark any more, nor fear the dangers of the day; nor dread the plagues of darkness, nor disasters in the morning' (Psalm 91:5–6), and as I prayed, a sense of calm came over me. Soon, as I drove, the welcoming lights of a service station loomed up. How I thanked God as I drove in, received directions, and was soon on a road that I recognised.

When I unlocked the door of my home and walked in I was overwhelmed with gratitude to God; not only for getting me safely home but also for something that up to that moment I had taken for granted. I had a deep awareness of how safe I felt in my own home – the blessedness of a roof over my head and my own four walls; such a sharp contrast to the vulnerability I'd experienced 'out there', alone on lonely roads leading to places I didn't know.

Life is a journey, and there cannot be a living person who has not taken wrong turnings and been lost. The good news is that Jesus is the Good Shepherd who came to seek out the lost, and who is always waiting to rescue us and guide us when we sincerely turn to Him for help.

Many years ago I had a dream I believe was from God. I was walking along a path with a destination in mind. Running alongside the path was a stream and beyond the stream a marsh. I knew that I must not get onto the marsh but suddenly, there I was, right in the middle of it, being sucked down and totally helpless.

Then, amazingly, I was lifted out of it and in my dream I *knew* that my rescuer was God Himself. I then had a wonderful sensation of skimming over the surface of the marsh and I felt that underneath were His everlasting arms. He set me down on the road, facing in the right direction.

When I thought about that dream I felt that God was assuring me that when I sincerely try to walk with Him I can trust Him to help me get back on track when I lose the way – which, being human, I can easily do! Psalm 119, verse 105 says, 'Your word is a lamp to my feet and a light for my path' (NIV).

Please help me Lord to keep Your Word in my heart and to remember that You promised to be with me always. Amen.

I feel lost

Father, I feel lost
Remote and far away.
I long to sense Your closeness
And in Your arms to stay.

Please let me know Your presence,
Please calm my wandering mind,
For your peace is the essence
Of all I need to find.

Help me Lord to watch with You,
To see things through Your eyes,
To have a heart that understands,
Please teach me to be wise.

Help me Lord to hear Your voice
And then do what You say,
To speak the word You give me
And by Your side to stay.

Dear Lord, You are my all in all,
I come to You today,
For You Lord are the potter
And I am but the clay.

22. *The power of words*

I once learnt a lesson from a pair of lace-up boots! The tongue of the right one just would not stay in place so, wearing them, I returned to the shop to demonstrate the problem. The manager assured me that it could be rectified. She asked me to bring the boot in at my convenience. This I did, and proceeded to tell my story to the girl at the counter who promptly called to the manager, 'It's the lady with the loose tongue.' For me that was an 'ouch' moment! The lady with the loose tongue. Am *I* really a lady with a loose tongue?

The Bible reminds us that life and death are in the power of the tongue, and in the letter of James it is likened to the small rudder which can steer a large ship (James 3:4). Such is the might of the tongue. How often I need to pray with the psalmist, 'Set a guard over my mouth, O LORD; keep watch over the door of my lips' (Psalm 141:3, NIV).

As children we used to chant, 'Sticks and stones may break my bones but words will never hurt me.' I now know that to be far from the truth. Words have enormous power to encourage and build up or to discourage and even destroy.

When I was eleven I was working desperately hard to win a scholarship to grammar school. One day, my teacher towered over me shouting, 'There'll be pigs flying in the sky the day *you* pass the scholarship.' I froze with fear and became very unwell, so much so that my mother took me to the doctor who said that

I was run down and needed a rest from school. Far from being delighted I was terrified and dared to say, 'I can't stay off school, I'm doing the scholarship.' A tonic was prescribed and, with the vision of flying pigs ever before me, I returned to the misery of the scholarship class. Surprisingly, I *did* pass the scholarship but on being given the news I burst into uncontrollable tears; surely a release from the fear those words had implanted.

Encouragement, on the other hand, can put courage into fearful hearts. And the beautiful reality is that every one of us can be an encourager. We speak what is in our hearts and so it behoves us to watch what we receive *into* our hearts. If we spend time reading and meditating on God's Word we are receiving words of life which we, in turn, can impart to others.

And on the most practical of levels we all have two guards over our tongues – our teeth and our lips!

Please help me Lord to watch over my heart allowing You to purify it so that the words I speak will bring life and not death. Amen.

23. *Your heart's desire*

When I was about eight my heart's desire was to be the proud possessor of the latest thing in brooches. These brooches were diamanté creations, each one in the shape of a letter of the alphabet. The idea was that you wore your own initial, glittering with diamonds! There they shone on Woolworth's counter – and they cost sixpence! Several of the 'posh' girls at school flaunted these exquisite things and I passionately yearned for one. My mother knew how much I wanted a diamanté brooch, and I hoped and prayed that on my birthday I'd be able to go to school wearing *my* initial in diamonds.

Life was hard for my parents. They really struggled to make ends meet. But my dear mother *did* buy me a sixpenny diamanté brooch from Woolworth's. The tragedy was that she didn't get me an initial brooch. She bought me one in the shape of a crescent moon with a pearl in the centre. I can see it now! I can also feel the disappointment which I had to hide. I really took no pleasure in my brooch because it wasn't what my heart desired. What a sad little tale.

I can think of other things for which I yearned as a child. As I recall them I realise that, when I longed for something, I *really* longed for it and nothing else could be a substitute. Fur-backed gauntlet gloves were another magnificent obsession, and I remember desperately wanting a box of chocolates with a picture of Shirley Temple on the lid!

Later on, of course, my heart's desires were for people – the first falling in love, the longing for it to be returned – and the pain when that did not happen.

As I think about the intensity of my desires in my childhood and youth, I ask myself this question: 'Marie, do you desire to know and to love God with that passionate intensity?'

It grieves me to admit that I don't have the passion for Jesus I want to have. I want to love Him *passionately*. I often think of His words in Revelation (Revelation 3:16), where He says He will spit the lukewarm out of His mouth. I cannot *bear* to be lukewarm. What am I to do? I believe the answer comes in verse 17, where Jesus says the lukewarm are trusting in themselves, and what they have, and they don't realise their need of Him. He invites us to go to Him, to humble ourselves at the foot of the cross and to be clothed in the garment of salvation.

I know that the more time I spend in the Word and in fellowship with God, the more open to God my spirit becomes, and my heart softens towards God. If I neglect my time with Him then *I* am the loser. I know it. Time spent devoted to God is something we will never regret. I remember the words of Jesus to Martha: '... Mary has chosen what is better, and it will not be taken away from her' (Luke 10:42, NIV). As we learn to sit at His feet, like Mary we find that our hearts and minds are drawn to Him and our love for Him will grow.

In Acts 4:13 we are told people marvelled at the confidence of Peter and John, and recognised that they had been with Jesus. How beautiful! Don't *you* desire to have that 'family resemblance'? Our Father longs to see many sons and daughters brought to glory. If we are faithful to our time with Him, He will change our hard hearts and we will find we are gradually becoming passionate about God. To know and love Him will become our heart's desire. Jesus says, 'Look! I have been standing at the door and I am constantly knocking. If anyone hears me calling him and opens the door, I will come in and fellowship with him and he with me' (Revelation 3:20).

Better is one day in your courts
than a thousand elsewhere;
I would rather be a doorkeeper in the house of my God
than dwell in the tents of the wicked.
For the LORD God is a sun and shield;
*   the LORD bestows favour and honour;*
no good thing does he withhold
from those whose walk is blameless.
O LORD Almighty,
*   blessed is the man who trusts in you.*
Psalm 84:10–12, NIV

24. *The sands of time*

When I was a child my birthday was a wonderful
occasion. I'm amazed as I look back to realise the lengths
to which my parents went in order to make our birthdays
so special, even though we were such a big family. At the
age of nine I had five younger siblings – and four more
babies were yet to be born! Times were hard.
Nevertheless, when our birthdays came round we knew
we'd receive a present (sixpence worth of something from
Woolworth's!). We knew we'd receive a birthday card and
that there'd be a party – just ourselves plus two others,
both only children whom my mother had a big enough
heart to invite to the feast. And a feast it was. There was
the essential birthday cake with candles, plus chocolate
cake, lemon-curd tarts, jelly and custard and other
delicious sweet treats, all baked by my mother.

As the big day approached my anticipation and excitement
escalated. The days were counted off. The day came. Everything
happened that I knew would happen. But I also clearly
remember the sadness I felt at the end of the day. Why? Because
I'd have to wait for a whole year until my next birthday!

How differently I feel today! The years seem to pass with
ever-increasing speed and I no longer look forward to being a
year older. As I look in the mirror I'm reminded time is running
out and that one of my birthdays will be the last.

Perhaps now is the time to discover whether we need to make

some changes in the time God has given us. We enter the world with nothing and we leave it with nothing. Between our birthday and our 'death day' our lives are lived and timed. Of course we need a calendar, which enables us to have a degree of order in our lives, but are we in control of our use of time or are we on a ruthless treadmill? What we do with our time determines the kind of person we become.

Jesus told the story of a businessman who gave differing amounts of money to three servants to invest during his absence. The first two used their time well and gave their master a good return but the third wasted his time and had nothing to show for it. Their master rewarded the first two but punished the lazy steward (Matthew 25:14–30).

Verses 15 and 16 in Psalm 139 say:

> *You were there while I was being formed in utter seclusion! You saw me before I was born and scheduled each day of my life before I began to breathe. Every day was recorded in your Book!*

Dear Lord, please help me to live each day as You would have me live it, doing Your will and for Your glory. For at the end of my life I long to hear You say, 'Well done, My good and faithful servant.'

25. *Little things mean a lot*

Some little things remain BIG in my memory. For instance there's the occasion when my companion asked me if I'd like a cola. 'I think I would,' was my reply. 'I'm paying for this,' he said, producing his wallet with a flourish. Why did my heart melt? Because my benefactor was my nine-year-old grandson, Sam! At about the same age, he once walked across the sitting room and gave me 20p to spend!

Another heart-melting moment happened just three months after the death of my husband. It was Valentine's Day. Imagine my surprise when my fifteen-year-old granddaughter Rachel arrived, bringing a card which she'd made for me. Such kind thoughtfulness! I confess I've saved all the cards I've received from children; their blotches and mistakes make them all the more precious.

I would guess we've all been recipients of small gifts or acts of kindness which have blessed us out of all proportion to their actual worth, simply because of the motivation which prompted them. One cannot measure the value of these seemingly small things. For how can one measure the depth of love? All we know is that our hearts respond.

Could this be a small reflection of our heavenly Father's response as we offer our gifts to Him? *Our* gifts – but who gave us those gifts? In the letter of James we read, 'Every good and perfect gift is from above, coming down from the Father of the heavenly lights, who does not change like shifting shadows' (James 1:17, NIV).

I'm reminded of a child who receives his pocket-money. The money is now his, but he chooses to spend some of it on a Christmas present for his parents. The gift delights them even though they were the providers, because it speaks of their child's love for them.

And so I believe it is with God. Every good thing we have is a gift from Him. As we offer Him our little love gifts of praise, worship, money, work – yes, even our lives – we delight His Father heart. The Bible says, 'Whatever you do, work at it with all your heart, as working for the Lord, not for men' (Colossians 3:23, NIV). As we do, I sense He sees the love in our hearts, accepts our gift and smiles on us. A chord of love resounds between God and us and, as the Bible tells us, love never fails (1 Corinthians 13:8).

Heavenly Father, I thank You for the gifts You have given to me. Please help me to use them as You wish them to be used, and also to remember that a little is a lot if it's all I've got and I give it to Jesus. Amen.

26. *Our personal screens*

In this age of technology I feel somewhat of a dinosaur and, whilst acknowledging computers can do amazing feats, I do not like them!

I'll try to explain myself. I see the computer as a powerful tool for good or evil, depending upon the one handling the mouse. And even in a 'good hand', it can dangerously monopolise one's life: too many hours spent focusing on that screen have the effect of secluding us from people. Relationships almost inevitably suffer. Perhaps every computer should have a warning notice – 'Use With Care'! My belief is that God made us for relationships; first with Himself, and then with each other.

It concerns me greatly when I hear about the hours many children spend alone in their rooms, alone with a computer. Whilst recognising that it is an essential tool for the child of today, surely safeguards, priorities and balance need to be established.

A school in the Northeast of England carried out an interesting experiment some years ago. The staff were concerned about the children's general behaviour. They decided to introduce them to the old playground games and rhymes: ring games, skipping games, ball games, clapping games and so on. Result? The children loved them and there was a marked improvement in their behaviour. What was the cause of such an interesting and encouraging outcome? I think it was because they were learning to relate, to take turns, to be fair, to see that they needed each other and, yes, to enjoy each other as they did things together.

I believe that the quality of our lives is defined by our relationships. As Jesus said, "'Love the Lord your God with all your heart and all your soul and with all your mind." This is the first and greatest commandment. And the second is like it: "Love your neighbour as yourself"' (Matthew 22:37–39, NIV).

As I thought about that, it dawned on me that we each have a screen before us. We wake in the morning and look at the day ahead or sometimes the week, the month or the year. We see the people, the circumstances, the tasks. It's all too easy to be busy, darting here and there. Perhaps our heavenly Father is watching our antics and longing for us just to STOP, be still and let His hand cover ours, guiding us to what *He* would have us do.

Lord, as I look upon the screen for the day, please help me to be wise in the choices I make. Amen.

27. *The beloved son*

Baron Fitzgerald, a wealthy Englishman, had only one child, a son. Tragically, while the boy was in his early teens his mother died: a few years later, the boy also died.

The baron's wealth was contained in his wonderful collection of works of art. Instructions were left in his will that on his death everything had to be sold by auction. Time went by, the baron died and the world of curators and collectors assembled for the pre-auction viewing. Amongst the great paintings was a portrait of the baron's son. It was of poor quality, having been painted by a local artist and was of no interest to the experts.

The auctioneer then read from the baron's will – it said the portrait of his beloved son had to be put up for auction first. Because the experts saw no value in it there was a distinct lack of interest; only one bid was received and that came from an old servant who had dearly loved the boy. He bought the painting for less than a pound. The auctioneer then dramatically stopped the auction and asked the lawyer to read from the will again. This is what he read: 'Whoever buys the painting of my son gets *all* of my art collection; the auction is over.' It's impossible to imagine the shock this announcement must have caused, or the regret in the minds and hearts of the experts. And as for the old servant – what an *amazing* and unexpected gift! His heart must have been overwhelmed with gratitude.

As I think of the derision with which the art experts viewed the portrait of the baron's son, my heart is stirred for I remember the contempt with which Jesus, the Son of God, was viewed by so many during His life on this earth, climaxing in the mockery He endured as He hung on the cross.

The message of the cross is that God's Son willingly took our sin upon Himself – and the punishment we deserve. Let us not be contemptuous and thereby lose the opportunity of receiving God's gift. His free gift of forgiveness is truly an amazing grace which is offered to all who will accept God's Son, Jesus, as their Saviour and their Lord.

In his second letter to the Corinthians (2 Corinthians 8:9), Paul writes: 'You know how full of love and kindness our Lord Jesus was: though he was so very rich, yet to help you he became so very poor, so that by being poor he could make you rich.'

Heavenly Father, thank You for the gift of Jesus. Please forgive our pride, our contempt, our lukewarm attitudes. As we look upon Your Son Jesus, may our hearts be broken open to receive Your amazing grace. Amen.

28. *The crossword*

For many people, the solving of the daily crossword is a magnificent obsession.

At one time in my life *I* almost became addicted. The clues, of course, were vital, as was my attention to them if I were to solve the puzzle. How it pleased me when I saw the answer instantly. And equally, how frustrated I was when I just couldn't get it. It used to surprise me, however, that if I returned to it later I often immediately got the word that had been escaping me.

I have to admit that I wasn't very good at crosswords and often resorted to the dictionary, the atlas, or the brains of any unsuspecting soul who arrived on the scene. I simply *had* to get that puzzle solved!

How surprising that we can spend so much time trying to solve a crossword puzzle and yet drift through our days without paying real attention to the clues God has given us to help us solve the puzzle of life itself.

The most sobering fact that every living being must face is that life as we know it will come to an end. The question arises: 'Is death the end?' And then the inner protestation: 'There must be *more* than this!' The Bible tells us God has set eternity in the heart of man (Ecclesiastes 3:11) which I believe is why we ask such questions of ourselves and possibly of others. Deep down we want to know the answers to these mysteries. *Has* God given us clues? I believe He has, but it is necessary to stop drifting and to apply diligence to finding the solutions to the puzzle of life;

surely far more important than the daily crossword puzzle!

In Paul's letter to the Romans (1:19–20) we read that God has put the knowledge of Himself into our hearts and that from earliest times men have seen the earth and the sky and all God made, and have known of His existence and great eternal power. God's creation! God's power! And as I recall some of the words of Carl Gustav Boberg's wonderful 1885 hymn, '*Oh Lord my God! When I in awesome wonder/Consider all the works Thy hand hath made,*' I too can but say, '*How great Thou art!*'

The Bible, Paul says, 'was given to us by inspiration from God and is useful to teach us what is true and to make us realise what is wrong with our lives; it straightens us out and helps us to do what is right' (2 Timothy 3:16). It is often referred to as the Word of God and through the Bible we meet Jesus, the Word made flesh, or the living Word. We read in the Bible of the cross on which Jesus died so that we can have eternal life, now and after death, if we will put our trust in Him. So – the cross of Jesus and the Word of God. They are the solution to the puzzle of the crossword of life.

There is no end to what God will teach us if we spend time daily seeking His wisdom and help in life's journey. It is a wonderful way to live.

Thank You, dear Lord, for Your cross and Your Word – the Living Word, Jesus, and Your written Word, the Bible. The cross and the Word solve the puzzle of life. Please help me to diligently seek You, for Your Word says, 'Come near to God and he will come near to you' (James 4:8, NIV). Amen.

29. *A clean page*

As a scholarship girl at grammar school my books and stationery were all provided: all, that is, except 'The Jotter'. The jotter was essential, for into it went all notes of lessons, homework assignments, and the tests which could be sprung upon us at any time. This very ordinary exercise book could be purchased at Woolworth's for three pence. Nothing in that, you may be thinking, but I assure you it was a big *something* in *my* life. As I got near to the last page, my anxiety would increase. It may be incomprehensible in this age of plenty, but I knew that my mother really could not spare the necessary three pence. And so I used to erase the work on the last few pages and re-use them, thus delaying the moment when I would have to admit that I needed a new jotter. The grubbiness of those pages bothered me and I tried to hide from other eyes what I was having to resort to. I felt ashamed, all the more keenly because my other exercise books were models of clean, beautiful writing and presentation. I took pride in them and enjoyed the praise from my teachers.

Life can be compared to a book – each one's life a fascinating story, and each day a page in that story.

For the greater part of my life I was striving to be perfect in the hope of earning my salvation. I was afraid of going to hell and therefore hoped I would make it into heaven! Slightly reminiscent, perhaps, of the efforts I made to present beautiful written work to my teachers in order to win praise and not punishment. But, of course, my efforts to live a sinless life were hopeless. Day after day I failed and at the end of each day I was only too well aware of my sins, reminiscent of the grubby pages of the jotter.

What a blessed relief when I began to understand that salvation is a gift from God – I cannot earn it. I don't have to carry the grubbiness of yesterday's sin into today. As I confess my sins and ask His forgiveness, He forgives me and His precious blood cleanses me. Each day can be a clean page.

The poet and hymnwriter, William Cowper wrote:

> *There is a fountain fill'd with blood,*
> *Drawn from Emmanuel's veins;*
> *And sinners plung'd beneath that flood*
> *Lose all their guilty stains.*

Every day can be a fresh beginning. Alleluia.

'Now all praise to God for his wonderful kindness to us and his favor that he has poured out upon us, because we belong to his dearly loved Son. So overflowing is his kindness towards us that he took away all our sins through the blood of his Son, by whom we are saved; and he has showered down upon us the richness of his grace – for how well he understands us and knows what is best for us at all times.' (Ephesians 1:6–8)

30. *Jean and Steven*

Some years ago my friend Jean rang me to say that her son, Steven, who was twenty-four, was ill.

Jean, a retired nurse, had been concerned for Steven for some months, sensing something was wrong with her lovely son. Eventually he was seen by their doctor, who arranged his immediate admission to hospital. Tests were conducted, and almost at once a dreadful diagnosis was given: Steven had new variant CJD, a fatal degenerative disease. I couldn't imagine how Jean felt but I clearly remember my own shock and horror as she gave me the terrible news, knowing that my feelings were a very pale reflection of hers. She knew this was a cruel death sentence on her handsome, athletic, gentle son, and she had a nurse's understanding of what they were facing.

How did Jean cope with such a tragedy? I have her permission to share with you how she walked through the dark valley. After the initial shock and sense of horror, Jean realised that she had two deep desires: a woman of deep Christian faith, she longed for Steven to receive the love and peace of Jesus into his heart. That was her first prayer. The second was that she would be able, with her nursing skills, to care for Steven herself.

Many people prayed for them. We all knew that God can and does work miracles, and how grateful we would have been had Steven been miraculously healed. But this was not to be, for within five months Steven had died. And yet, throughout this hard time we could see that prayers were being answered, for

Steven *did* receive the love and peace of Jesus, and for the most part Jean nursed him herself. Steven died peacefully at home with his mother praying beside him. Her strength, faith, love and courage were remarkable, and I could simply look on and think, 'Only God could enable her to be like this.'

At Steven's funeral, the minister told of a little boy who discovered a bird's nest full of eggs. He was thrilled! This would be *his* secret, *his* nest. He would return as often as he could to look at it and this he did until the day when he arrived to find the shells cracked open and empty. Heartbroken, he ran home and sobbed out his sad story to his mother who comforted him and said to her little boy, 'Don't cry! The little birds were made to fly from their shells and be free. Be *glad* for them!'

And so it is for Steven. He is no longer trapped in a sick body but is with his Father in heaven where there is no more death, nor sorrow, nor crying, nor pain (Revelation 21:4). Furthermore, Jean's faith gives her the assurance that one day she too will be with Steven in that heavenly home.

Jesus, it is such a comfort to know that You feel with me when I am lost and at my most vulnerable. Please help me allow You to comfort me. Amen.

31. *Dividing walls*

I once read a story about a sailor who drowned and whose body was washed up on the beach of an island. It's said because the islanders believed he was of a different religion from them they buried his body outside the wall of their cemetery.

Years later, an ex-islander returned to visit the grave of her ancestors. She noticed, to her surprise, that the sailor was now buried *within* the cemetery and assumed his grave had been opened and his coffin re-interred within the wall. However, on making enquiries, she learnt that the decision had been made to demolish part of the cemetery wall and replace it with a new one so the sailor's remains could be included in their graveyard.

I see a heart-searching challenge in that story. Whilst walls of brick can divide us, there are dividing walls of a far more sinister nature.

Which of us has not suffered from being excluded? Our first such experience could have been in the school playground when we weren't allowed to join in a game. For others, rejection comes from within the home, damaging the core relationships on which our lives are built. Rejection drops deep into our hearts and a foundation is laid onto which the next hurt will settle and so it can go on. Sadly, we can go through life expecting and fearing rejection and so we build walls of protection around ourselves. As we exclude others from our lives we put ourselves into isolation, and ivory towers are lonely places! Not a pleasant way to live. By contrast, Psalm 133 declares, 'How good and pleasant it is when brothers live together in unity!' (v.1).

So can we dismantle the dividing walls we ourselves have erected? I believe we can. It usually demands of us large doses of humility and forgiveness, and a good helping of prayer, plus a willingness to look for and use opportunities creatively.

In his letter to the Philippians, Paul writes, 'Then make me truly happy by loving each other and agreeing wholeheartedly with each other, working together with one heart and mind and purpose' (Philippians 2:2). Humanly speaking, a difficult goal, but with God's Holy Spirit dwelling in us, and our willingness to obey, nothing is impossible.

Lord, show me if I have put up walls in my relationships with others, and help me now to pull them down. However hard this may seem, I can do it because You are with me. Amen.

His broken body

I wonder what the tree was like;
The tree that through the years grew tall,
The tree that was felled, and roughly hewn,
The tree that became the cross.

I wonder where the ironstone lay;
The iron that lay in the earth,
The iron that was melted and battered into shape,
The iron that became those nails.

I wonder what the bush was like;
The bush which bore the thorns,
Those thorns that were roughly stripped away,
The thorns that became that crown.

I wonder what those men were like;
Those men who crucified our Lord;
And I wonder, as dismayed I see
Those men were just like you and me.

For even now don't we break His body
When dividing walls we build
Between ourselves and 'different' others
But all dearly loved by Him?

Forgive us, Lord, for our lack of love.
You prayed we would all be one.
As we hear that prayer we yield our wills
And say may Your will be done.

32. *The King's gate*

Mark Stibbe, former vicar of St Andrew's, Chorley Wood, and now leader of the Father's House Trust, in his beautiful book, *The Father You've Been Waiting For* (Authentic Media, 1996), tells of his own conversion to Christianity.

Mark had a privileged education at Winchester College, a place with a history of outstanding academic success but where, in his day, it definitely was not cool to be a committed Christian!

However, in 1976 there was powerful move of God in the school. Mark describes seeing some of his own rebellious friends becoming Christians and their lives being transformed Mark resisted for as long as he could but on 17 January 1977 a strange thing happened. Whilst walking down Kingsgate Street, looking at the stars and repeating to himself a line from a track on a Pink Floyd album, *Is There Anybody Out There?* Mark sensed a voice in his heart saying, 'Yes'. This was followed by a question: 'And if you died tonight where would you stand before the judgment throne of God?'

In a flash, he was convicted of the awesome holiness of God, that we live in a moral universe, that we are all accountable for our actions and that he had been living a self-centred life. Mark knew in that moment he needed God's forgiveness and a Saviour, so he could be sure of heaven when he died. Without delay, he ran to the house of the teacher who ran the Christian group and just before midnight he said a prayer, choosing to follow Jesus for the rest of his life. By God's grace, thirty years later, Mark's life is still under the Lordship of Jesus Christ.

Because I live in the beautiful city of Winchester I frequently walk down Kingsgate Street and through the King's Gate. The thought of Mark's conversion often comes to me and I recall that it was here that he found the gateway to his King. In John's Gospel (John 10:9), Jesus says, 'I am the gate; whoever enters through me will be saved.' How wonderful a promise is that?

Jesus, You said that no one comes to the Father except through You. Thank You for being our gate to eternal life. Amen.

33. *Seeing Jesus in people*

Have you ever been overwhelmed by sadness and fear?
I would guess we all have. Perhaps it helps to remember
that even Jesus experienced those feelings, such as in the
Garden of Gethsemane the night before His crucifixion.
We know that after the greatest travail a soul could endure
He said to His heavenly Father, 'Yet not what I will, but
what you will' (Mark 14:36, NIV).

We read in the Bible that whilst David was being pursued by
Saul he lost his position, his money, his wife – everything, and
was driven to hiding in caves (1 Samuel 23). How humbling is
that? There he cried to God for help: 'Hear my cry, for I am very
low. Rescue me from my persecutors, for they are too strong
for me. Bring me out of prison, so that I can thank you. The
godly will rejoice with me for all your help' (Psalm 142:6–7).
He was thanking and praising whilst still in the cave! I heard a
wonderful sermon based on this biblical event: the recurring
message was 'God does His best work in the cave, for He is
with us'. The cave experience comes to us all at some time in
our lives and I know I draw closer to God and grow spiritually
through the hard things that happen.

Many years ago, my late husband, Arthur, and I were 'in a
cave'. Things were bad. We prayed and wept together and if we
had to go out we went out together. Inevitably, the day came
when I had to go out on my own. I prayed and said, 'Jesus, You'll
have to walk with me … *please!*' As I emerged from the house

I saw a little man just about to mount his bike but when he saw me he waited and walked with me.

Now, I have to confess that I'd always thought this man very boring and if at all possible I had avoided his company. Imagine how I felt as I remembered my prayer and realised that Jesus *was* walking with me in the person of this man. I was humbled that day. God used my desperation to teach me an important lesson. In my brokenness He sent me help through the most unlikely person.

He is the God of surprises. Did He not send His Son Jesus to be born in a stable and to die on a cross? How unlikely is that?

Dear Lord, please help me to recognise Your hand on my life, to see You in others and to be humble, thinking of others as better than myself. Amen.

34. *Hearing God's voice*

I remember the amazement a friend expressed when first being fitted with a hearing-aid. What seemed to give him most delight was that the device enabled him to hear the birdsong in the trees.

He told me he'd thought that they had stopped singing! Of course they hadn't, but he had stopped hearing. Deafness is a hard thing to bear because it impedes communication, and is potentially cruelly isolating.

I believe we can all suffer from a spiritual deafness, which blocks our communication with God. In Psalm 95 we read, 'Oh, that you would hear him calling you today and come to him!' (Psalm 95:7). Just as the birds have not stopped singing, God has not stopped speaking.

My son Richard once introduced me to a volunteer in a soup kitchen for the homeless, a young man called Tony. I told him about a radio programme I'd heard that day in which it was suggested that charities encouraged people to be scroungers. His view was that there are scroungers in all walks of life, citing people who evade paying their taxes, and those who make money in dishonest ways, as two examples. He went on to say it was not his place to judge people. Jesus had given him compassion for the homeless, so whether they realised it or not, they were coming into contact with the love of Jesus when they came into the soup kitchen.

He then told us of a recent happening. At the end of a night's work they had one meal left over. A volunteer asked if he could take it home for his dog. Tony was on the point of agreeing when he sensed that he should refuse, saying, 'No. This meal is for someone.' As he drove home through the darkened streets he noticed a man turning into an alleyway. Stopping the van, he called, 'Do you want a meal?' The man turned, looked into his face and said, 'I believe Jesus has sent you.' He explained he'd had no food for two and a half days and in desperation had cried, 'Jesus, if You're really there, please send me some food.' And He did, through Tony, who recognised God's prompting.

God speaks to us in different ways; perhaps through the vivid beauty of a sunset, the glorious majesty of a mountain, the sweet perfume of a flower, or the wonder of a newborn baby. As we are stirred by God's creation, we can respond with thanks and praise.

Sometimes the meaning of a verse from Scripture drops down from head to heart and suddenly we understand; our hearts are grateful. Or we hear that gentle prompting by the Holy Spirit as Tony did.

And most dearly, God speaks to us through the life and words of His beloved Son Jesus who said, 'My sheep recognise my voice, and I know them, and they follow me' (John 10:27).

How do we get to know anyone? By spending time with them: communicating with them. And so it is with God. How wise and blessed we are if we have a daily date with our Creator, who marvellously is also our Father.

Help us, Lord, to order our days so that we spend quiet time with You, alone. Amen.

Was that You, Lord?

Was that You, Lord?
Did You speak?
Would You speak to me?
Can it be true, Lord
That You care?
That You want to talk to me?

I believe You do,
But what about me?
Do I listen?
Dare I listen?
How often I just haven't time,
How often I just don't believe.

What sadness,
What incredible sadness,
That the child in whom You delight
Has other things to do
And really hasn't time for You.
And yet You wait.

Lord, I want to stop spinning plates.
Please help me to stop,
To sit at Your feet
And listen.

35. *The clanging of the gates*

I was evacuated at the outbreak of the Second World War. I have vivid memories of my evacuation on 8 September 1939. It coincided with my first day at the grammar school, to which I had just been awarded a scholarship. I had to arrive there carrying a suitcase, a gas mask, and wearing full winter uniform: tunic, blouse and tie, woollen stockings, winter coat, velour hat and gloves – the lot – and it was a very hot day!

We assembled in the school hall, were given a pep talk about good manners and then, lining up in fours, we walked down the centre of the road towards the railway station. I remember that many parents were walking on the pavements, some of them endeavouring to keep apace with us. Letting their children go in such uncertain circumstances must have been so painful. In my childish mind I had no understanding of the horrors of war, but our parents, whose lives had already been darkened by the Great War, would be well aware of the horrendous possibilities. The worst scenario, of course, being that they might never see their children again.

On arrival at the station we were shepherded onto the platform – still in our lines of four. Suddenly, a very frightening thing happened – huge, iron gates were drawn across the gap which separated parents and children. They clanged with a deafening finality. We could see parents desperately trying to catch a last glimpse of us; they had made a hard decision on our behalf in order to give us the best chance in life, but it was very painful for us all.

The memory of those clanging gates reminds me of a story Jesus told in the Gospel of Luke. He spoke of a hard-hearted rich man and a poor beggar named Lazarus. After death the beggar is seen with Abraham but the rich man is in torment. He pleads for help from Lazarus but Abraham says, ' … between us and you a great chasm has been fixed, so that those who want to go from here to you cannot, nor can anyone cross over from there to us' (Luke 16:19–31, NIV).

A moment will come for each of us when we no longer have another chance to make a choice. Those who have put their faith in Jesus for their salvation will be filled with unutterable joy. But just as those iron gates formed an insurmountable barrier so there will be no crossing the great divide after death.

Oh God, have mercy on me. Help me to choose to put my trust in Jesus' perfect sacrifice on my behalf. Help me to receive salvation while I am able to make a choice. Amen.

The safest place

God of earth and sky and sea,
God of the universe,
Thou hast created me
And as I come to Thee
I'm filled with awe
To think that Thou dost know me.
Thou knowest me and yet
Thou lovest me.

My sins O Lord – they wounded Thee,
My heart weeps with sorrow
For sin is always at my door
And yet – Thy grace is more.
Thy tears of compassion weep on me.
Thy fountain of blood cleanses me,
Thy river of grace forgives me
And I am in a safe place,
Enfolded in Thine arms of love,
Gazing into Thine eyes of love,
And like a little child –
I am content.

Help me to run to Thee
Often and often –
To whisper words of love to Thee
And to hear Thine amazing
Words of love to me.

36. *Prayer*

A little girl was seriously ill and surgery was necessary to save her life.

As she lay on the operating table, the surgeon said to her, 'In order to make you better, I'll need to put you to sleep.' 'Oh,' said the child, 'if I am going to sleep I must say my prayers.' She closed her eyes, joined her hands and said a prayer which I guess many of us said as children: 'As I lie on my bed to sleep, to God I give my soul to keep, and if I die before I wake, to God I give my soul to take. In Jesus' name. Amen.'

The surgeon later confessed he prayed that night for the first time in thirty years. The example of a little child, so simple yet profound, had touched his heart and he responded in the way for which his heavenly Father had been waiting. Jesus once said that unless we turn from our sins and become as little children we cannot enter the kingdom of heaven (Matthew 19:14; Mark 10:15; Luke 18:16).

In the aftermath of the attacks on the Twin Towers on 11 September 2001, so many people turned to God. People prayed. Churches were full. The important things of life were thought about and talked about.

In today's culture intellect, physique and possessions have become more important than the life of the spirit. Advertising urges us on to achieve the body beautiful, the ideal home, the lifestyle that gives us what we want, when we want it. As these things monopolise our attention our spirits are neglected.

Consequently we lose faith in, and contact with, our Creator; and, as a light goes out when the power is cut, so our spirits dim as we ignore God's presence and power.

To get to know other human beings it is necessary to spend time with them. So it is with God. It is the most amazing reality that Almighty God longs to hear us speaking to Him, and not just when we're desperate! Even more amazing is that *He* speaks to *us*. We have an 'open line' to Him: no automated messages, no being put on hold, but straight through to our heavenly Father and to Jesus.

I once heard someone say that the one thing we won't regret when we come before God for judgment is the time we 'wasted' being quiet in His presence while here on earth. Pressures come at us from all directions, and with them the thoughts of all we could or feel we should be doing. But God says, 'Be still, and know that I am God' (Psalm 46:10). As I respond to His invitation and start my day in this way, I have confidence that He will lead me to the work He has for me to do.

Jesus, You were a man of prayer. Thank You for the prayer You taught us, the Lord's prayer. Please help me to be faithful to my daily date with You. Amen.

Heart to heart

Christ's body, born in a stable,
It was there that He took his first breath.
'Midst the straw and the beasts
And the humble poor,
As He opened His eyes,
That's what He saw;
His first sight of this earth as a baby,
Even though as God in heaven
He'd seen it all before.

Christ's body died, pinned to a cross,
It was there that He took His last breath.
'Midst the blood and the pain
And the mocking of men
As He gazed with His eyes,
That's what He saw;
His last sight of this earth as a man,
Even though as God in heaven
He'd seen it all before.

Why? I ask You Jesus, why?

Dear one, it was the way I chose
To make a way for you,
To set you free from sin and death
And bring you home to Me.
My grace will open your eyes
And then your heart will see
That from the wood of the manger
To the wood of the cross
You were in My heart.

Is there room in yours for Me?

37. *Misunderstandings*

So much trouble is caused through misunderstandings and I sense that many relationships might have been saved had time and care been taken to explain things. For instance, a lady admired the photograph of the young boy of the family she was visiting. 'My mum doesn't like it,' said the child. 'Why do you think that?' asked their visitor. 'Well, she's going to have it blown up,' he replied. Not quite what his mother had in mind!

Then there's the story of the young lad who rang his mother to tell her that he'd just broken a vase in the home of his friend. Trying to reassure her he added, 'But you don't need to buy one because his mother said it's irreplaceable.' Ouch!

I once overheard a thought-provoking conversation between two of my grandsons; Ben was six and Sam was three. 'Are you a Christian, Sam?' Ben asked. After a moment's pause came Sam's reply: 'I don't know.' A reflective silence was followed by Ben's solution: 'All you have to do is give your heart to Jesus.' Sam thought and then said, 'I can't do that because if I did I'd be dead.' It was time for Ben's dad to step in and explain what was meant by giving one's heart to Jesus – and to assure Sam a surgeon's knife would *not* be involved!

I gave my heart to Jesus when the truth of the gospel message reached my heart. It is summed up by John in his first letter. Speaking of Jesus, he said, 'He is the one who took God's wrath against our sins upon himself, and brought us into fellowship with God; and he is the forgiveness for our sins, and not only ours but all the world's' (1 John 2:2). God so loved *me* that He gave His Son Jesus to me as the way of bringing me back to Himself. And Jesus then gave His *life* for me. How could I not love such a Father and such a Saviour and not offer my heart, my life?

Another term that is often misunderstood is 'born-again Christian'. All true Christians *are* born again. Jesus Himself was the first person to use the term when speaking to Nicodemus, a religious Jew who was seeking the truth. Jesus told him that it is necessary to be born again by the work of the Holy Spirit, bringing His life into our spirits before we can enter God's kingdom (John 3:1–15).

The words we use can build bridges of understanding or dividing walls of misunderstanding. That is surely an awesome responsibility! An important lesson I've learnt is that I should never assume things. I've learnt it the hard way, having often been proved wrong in my assumptions. How much better to take the time to listen and to explain.

Lord, I am sorry for walls of division that I have helped erect. Please help me to restore damaged relationships and give me the grace to watch my words that they may be bridge builders. Amen.

38. *Separation*

One of the most awful moments of my childhood was when my baby brother Jim, just twenty-two months old, was diagnosed with scarlet fever. I was eight and adored him. As we waited for the dreaded 'fever van' to arrive, I sat crying.

In those days, scarlet fever meant total isolation, and my parents could only watch Jim through a window. He had a hospital number, 1268, and it would be printed in the local daily paper and also posted outside the hospital under the appropriate heading, ranging from 'critically ill' to 'improving'. He was on the critically ill list for a long time. What agony for my parents to see their little baby so ill, so near to them and yet unable to touch him. What trauma for their little son too – shocked, ill, feeling lost and crying; my heart aches even now as I think of it.

Another occasion I'll never forget was when my late husband and I took care of our little granddaughter Anna for about ten days. She was three and had chickenpox. Our daughter Miriam, Anna's mum, was at an important stage in attaining her Postgraduate Certificate in Education, so we took Anna the 120 miles to our home, confident that she would be happy with us as she knew us well. For the first week she seemed to be fine but I then became aware that Anna was pining. I went into her room one evening to find this tiny wisp of a girl sitting in the middle of a large bed, making no sound but with tears running down her face. I couldn't bear it. We quickly made arrangements to get Anna back to mum and dad. When I went in and told her the good news she clung to me passionately, laughing and then crying until all her pent-up emotion had been released.

Separation from loved ones is a very hard thing to bear. One can pine and become ill as one longs to see the loved one, to hear the voice, to feel the touch, to share the moments. When God breathed life into Adam he was actually pouring His heart of love into him. God desired an intimate life of love with Adam and all his descendants. His Father heart longed for sons and daughters who would enjoy continued fellowship with Him. Tragically, Adam separated himself from God through sin. He knew the consequence of disobedience would be death. God is not a cruel, vindictive taskmaster, but because He is love and wisdom, when He gives us a law it is for our own good. By separating himself from God, Adam died spiritually and he began to die physically. Death entered the human race.

As long as we remain separated from God we are pining inwardly. This is because we were made to be in union with Him. We try to find fulfilment in all sorts of ways but our souls will find no rest until we rest in Him. We find that rest through Jesus, the perfect obedient Son who died in our place, taking the punishment we deserve and thereby offering life and friendship with God to all who will receive Him as their Saviour.

Heavenly Father, Your love for me is so great that You allowed Yourself to be separated from Your beloved Son, Jesus, when He took my sin and the punishment that I deserve upon Himself. I thank You for the gift of Jesus. Please help me, through Him, to draw closer to You. Amen.

I'm hurting

Jesus, I hold my heart before You,
It's fragile and hurting and sad.
Dare I let go? Dare I entrust it
Into Your outstretched hand?

I know You invite me to do so,
You say to me, 'Do not fear'.
Will You really look after this heart
That is breaking, and give me
Your peace so dear?

Your love compels me to enter,
I let go of this crumbling mess,
You gently take hold and caress me
With Your love and Your tenderness.

39. *An attitude of gratitude*

A missionary was on a short trip to Tobago. On his final day, when he was leading the worship in a leper colony, he asked if anyone had a favourite song or hymn. A woman, with no ears, no nose, no lips and the most disfigured face he'd ever seen, raised her fingerless hand and asked, 'Could we sing *Count Your Blessings*'? The missionary started the song but, completely overcome, he couldn't finish it. When questioned later, he admitted he *would* sing that song again but never in the same way. That lady, from her seemingly impossible situation, was an inspiration. I would suggest that we should all practise expressing gratitude whatever the circumstances. There are always things for which to be grateful.

A famous Bible scholar, Matthew Henry, who lived 250 years ago, was robbed of all his money. In his diary, he wrote: 'First let me be thankful that I was never robbed before, second, because although they took my purse they did not take my life, third that, although they took my all, it was not much, and fourth because it was I who was robbed, not I who did the robbing.'

We can read in Acts 16 that because of their faith Paul and Silas had been thrown into prison and their feet put in the stocks. And yet, at midnight, they were praying and singing hymns of praise to God. What an attitude!

Our culture tells us we're entitled to everything we desire – and instantly! How foolish and impossible is that? But this insidious message seeps into our souls and when we don't get our own way we react like spoilt children, grumbling, 'It's not fair'.

As a user of public transport, I often have the opportunity to chat to strangers and to overhear conversations in the bus queue. I sometimes wonder: have we become a nation of grumblers? I've also learnt it's all too easy to go along with the moan, be it the bad weather or the late bus – there's always *something* that is not as we'd like it to be! It takes courage to swim against the tide.

Even in the hardest times there is much for which to be thankful. And I have discovered that as I do that – strangely – even if the *circumstances* appear to be unchanged, *I* am changed and blessed.

Finally, if ever I'm awake during the night, instead of counting sheep, I count my blessings from A to Z, thanking God for something or someone, beginning with each letter. Interestingly I rarely reach Z …

Father, we thank You that whatever our situation, we have so much for which to be grateful. Help us to recognise Your presence, Your provision, Your kindness. Amen.

40. *Feather beds!*

I became a Christian in the 1970s. How delighted I was to come into a personal relationship with God; to know Him as Abba – my Father. I was born again and a wonderful new life was just beginning, but as a baby Christian I had much to learn. For instance, I thought that I would receive from God everything I wanted – and quickly! What a lovely time I was going to have!

Certainly I saw some amazing answers to prayer when God graciously answered my requests with a quick 'yes'. One such occasion was unforgettable. Arthur and I needed £125 by a particular date in order to go to a Christian conference. For several weeks each morning I spoke out the verse from 2 Corinthians: 'And God is able to make all grace abound to you, so that in all things at all times, having all that you need, you will abound in every good work' (2 Corinthians 9:8, NIV), I would thank God for this promise. The day drew near, but nothing arrived. With only twenty-four hours until we were due to leave, there was still no money. Nevertheless, with faith we packed our bags. Then, with the last possible postal delivery before the conference, there came *five* Giro cheques each to the value of £125. We danced for joy! That experience was exceptional, and of course I had to learn that God's answer is sometimes 'no' or 'not yet', the reason being that He is omniscient and therefore knows the very best way of answering prayers. And this is when I put faith into action.

Psalm 91 verse 15 says, 'When he calls on me I will answer ...' And so it is that often I have to wait and to say, 'Lord, I don't understand but I will trust You and thank You.'

I once heard a priest say what namby-pamby Christians we'd be if we got everything we wanted straightaway. We would indeed be feeble, insipid, spoilt children and have you ever met a spoilt child who was contented? I think not.

I had a hard lesson to learn with my own children, especially as they were reaching adulthood and were making life choices. My desire for them was that their lives would be trouble-free, easy, pleasant and happy; all the usual things a loving mother would wish for her children. And of course they all had hard times to go through because, well, that's life. Then came the day when God spoke into my heart saying: 'Marie, you want your children to get to heaven on feather beds and it can't be so.' Of course He was right, being God! So I had to throw out the feather beds! Many years on I now can see that it's been in the hard times that I've grown closer to God.

And our heavenly Father knows how we feel. Did He not watch Jesus die on the cross? It is good for us to remember that when we, or our children or loved ones are suffering, He understands and suffers with us.

Dear Lord, help me not to get between You and those You have given me to love. Amen.

41. *Washing one another's feet*

Tearfund is a Christian charity dedicated to serving the poor in Third World countries. Their magazine cover once carried a photo of two feet caught in the motion of walking. They were the feet of 39-year-old Joyce Mbwilo who lived in a village in Tanzania.

Joyce had walked 14 miles a day every day for twenty-five years, not to keep fit and not to win a medal, but simply to collect water for her family. This worked out at over 5,000 miles a year, and she had walked the equivalent of three times round the world. How hard it is for us to imagine such a life. It humbles me as I realise how much I take for granted the running water in my home. Thank God that Tearfund has been able to help the local church to pipe water into Joyce's village.

The night before He died, Jesus wrapped a towel around His waist, poured water into a basin, washed His disciples' feet and dried them. He then said to them, 'And since I, the Lord and Teacher, have washed your feet, you ought to wash each other's feet. I have given you an example to follow: do as I have done to you. How true it is that a servant is not greater than his master. Nor is the messenger more important than the one who sends him. You know these things – now do them! That is the path of blessing' (John 13:14–17).

The picture of Joyce Mbwilo's feet, thick, leathery and dirt-ingrained is a symbol to us of a needy world; a world where one billion people live on less than one dollar a day.

Jesus once said, 'The poor you will always have with you ...' (Matthew 26:11).

I believe the challenge to us in our over-indulged Western world is this: how can we wash the feet of the needy? Certainly by giving our time and praying, but I believe it is incumbent upon us to share our wealth. Do we own it or does it own us? In his first letter to Timothy, Paul writes: 'For the love of money is the first step toward all kinds of sin. Some people have even turned away from God because of their love for it, and as a result have pierced themselves with many sorrows' (1 Timothy 6:10).

And Jesus Himself, speaking to the righteous on judgment day will say, 'When you did it to these my brothers you were doing it to me!'

Dear Lord, I invite You to examine my heart with me. Help me to be honest with myself and with You, regarding my possessiveness of possessions. Please help me to 'let go' and to bless others with my money. Amen.

42. *Where is your treasure?*

Have you ever been to a 'metal detecting' party? I guess not: Neither have I. But I do know someone who has! When my grandson Ben was eight he became fascinated with metal detecting, so for his ninth birthday he received a metal detector and, in conjunction with the store where it was purchased, his party was arranged. Can you imagine the scene? Ten excited boys, each with a detector, a field marked off into ten lanes and a buried treasure in each lane. Lovely, of course, that each boy found some treasure!

So, what *is* treasure to you and to me? How *hard* it is to be uncontaminated by the world's view on this. As I watch the TV shows where money is the prize, I realise what a powerful grip it has on people. The emotions exhibited following either a big win or loss tell their own story.

Then, of course, there is advertising which sows desire into hearts, and people are deceived into believing that buying bigger and better will bring happiness. It so often leads into a cruel financial trap, and indeed never really satisfies, for how quickly fashions change.

Jesus once said, 'Don't store up treasures here on earth where they can erode away or may be stolen. Store them in heaven where they will never lose their value, and are safe from thieves. If your profits are in heaven your heart will be there too' (Matthew 6:19–21).

On another occasion He said, 'The Kingdom of Heaven is

like a treasure a man discovered in a field. In his excitement, he sold everything he owned to get enough money to buy the field – and get the treasure, too!' (Matthew 13:44).

I was greatly challenged once when I visited a L'Abri Christian community group in Hampshire and saw a lifestyle diametrically opposed to our Western culture. There were a few staff whose main work was with students. We learned that the members of staff had all been in extremely well paid and prestigious positions, but had surrendered 'security' as we know it, responding to God's call to this work which, besides lecturing, included everything it takes to run a large establishment, from gardening and cooking to cleaning the loos. When we asked how the community was financed, the reply was, 'We live by faith; we never advertise, we never appeal: we pray.' We sensed a great peace there and I think they have found the pearl of great price.

Jesus wants us to find the truth about God, ourselves and the meaning of life – whatever the cost.

Dear Lord, please help me to have the wisdom to seek You until I find You. Amen.

Surrendering

My heart is hard
I would not have it so.
I hold it tightly
In a careful grip.
Why do I fear
To open and let go?
I hear my voice cry,
'But don't risk – what if?
What if you're left
With nothing in the bank?
What if you're taken
On an empty ride?'
What if? What if?
The scenes roll on and on.
Frightening indeed
If I do risk my all!

And then I look
Into His eyes of love,
The eyes of Him
Who risked His all for me.
I know He sees me,
Sees me as I am,
My wizened heart
Held tight so carefully.

His tears fall on me
Softening my heart
And so I dare
To loosen my strong hold.
For He who gave His all
Is melting my hard heart,
Inviting me
To answer to His call.

Dare I follow?
Lord, please give me grace
To trust You
As You lead the way.
With opening hands
And opening heart I pray
That You will gently mould me
Day by day.

43. *D-day*

D-day – 6 June 1944 – was one of the greatest land–sea operations in history. The Allied expeditionary force was carried across the English Channel in ships to crush the fighting power of the enemy. The minesweepers were in front, clearing a path for the flotilla that followed and facing bombs, torpedoes, gunfire, mines, E boats and destroyers.

On one of the minesweepers was a young man called Arthur Kane who, at seventeen, had volunteered to serve in the Royal Navy. For much of the war he had been a radar operator on the North Atlantic convoys, a hard war about which he was reluctant to speak. Ironically, D-day was Arthur's twenty-first birthday, the day on which he expected to die! Providentially, he survived and a decade later he and I met, and eventually we married.

In our young day the twenty-first was *the* big birthday when one was given the 'key of the door', symbolic of freedom. Freedom was important to Arthur – after all, he'd risked his life for it. Poignant indeed, that on the day when he should have been celebrating youth and life, he was facing the probability of death.

Arthur had an entrepreneurial and daring spirit. He was a very creative person who worked hard and was willing to take risks as he sought success in life. Yet success as he understood it did not come. Nothing really satisfied and neither of us knew why! That is, until we both experienced God's amazing grace through what was known as the charismatic renewal in the 1970s. God poured out His Holy Spirit across all the denominations and we were so blessed to be in a place where we were encouraged to receive His gift.

Because Arthur had been willing to lay down his life so that others could live, I feel he had a deep appreciation of what Jesus had done for him. Jesus had given *His* life so that Arthur could live, and Jesus became his hero. Only then did he find true freedom and peace. D-day had come for Arthur! The rest of his life was lived with Jesus at the centre.

Lord Jesus, the purpose of Your coming to earth was to lay down Your life to set mankind free. I thank You Jesus that You went to the cross for me. Please help me to offer up my life in obedience to You. Amen.

44. *The plodder*

I wonder whether you can remember the first time you heard a teacher talk about you? I can! I was a mere six years of age. My teacher was Miss Hardy and she was my idol! I thought she was beautiful. One day, whilst speaking to my mother, from her beautiful lips fell these words: 'Marie is a plodder.' I didn't like the sound of that! Why hadn't she said, 'Marie is bright' – or beautiful? But … a *plodder*?

Ah well, perhaps Miss Hardy was right! According to the dictionary, 'to plod' is to work slowly and perseveringly, and looking back over my life I think I have been just that, a plodder – never shining brilliantly, but eventually managing to reach my goals.

There are many goalposts on life's journey, and whilst some are obviously hugely important, others are seemingly small and unimportant. And yet I believe that the small things are important, too. In His parable about the talents, Jesus, speaking to the man who had been given the least but who had used it well, said, 'you are a good and faithful servant. You have been faithful over this small amount, so now I will give you much more' (Matthew 25:23). What an encouragement is that verse to us. Our gifts are precisely that: gifts from God, things we have not deserved.

In his letter to the Philippians, Paul writes, 'Forgetting the past and looking forward to what lies ahead, I strain to reach the end of the race and receive the prize for which God is calling us up to heaven because of what Christ Jesus did for us' (Philippians 3:13–14).

I have a friend who, at the age of sixty-seven, achieved his ambition of going to the Himalayas and doing the Annapurna Circuit (a 200–300 kilometre trek around the Annapurna mountain range in the Himalayas) climbing to a height of almost 18,000 feet, a fifteen-day trek. At 14,000 feet they spent three days acclimatising themselves to the thin air and then they pressed on, plodding to reach their goal. His guides carried his bags as the air got thinner, and my friend was crawling at the end: but he got there!

Here are two thoughts which may encourage us in this journey of perseverance. First, by perseverance, the snail reached the ark! Second, the usefulness of the postage stamp is its ability to stick to something until it gets there …

Actually I prefer being 'Marie the plodder' to being a snail or a postage stamp, but even they serve their purpose in bringing the message home.

Dear Jesus, thank You that You persevered up Calvary's hill to the cross. You did this so that I can press on to reach the home in heaven that You have prepared for me. I am forever grateful. Amen.

45. *The seeking Father*

Were our children particularly adventurous, or were we exceptionally careless parents? I don't know! But what I *do* know is this: we lost all four of them on different occasions, each of which is etched on my memory.

Miriam and John, aged three and two, took advantage of an unlocked back garden gate, left open by the dustbin men. They were found a few roads away holding hands and giggling. 'We were going to see Grandma,' they informed me, and actually, they *were* going the right way!

On to Richard, who at the age of five escaped into the crowds at Whitby harbour one August Bank Holiday Monday. We found him peering into deep water, his feet teetering over the edge of the harbour! And then there was Paul, who always liked to hold my hand, and who unexpectedly went missing at a large music festival. Panic reigned until we found him in the hut for lost children.

Many parents tell equally traumatic tales of such heart-stopping moments, when fear gripped and minds seemed to freeze. And just as passionately, we remember the inexpressible relief and joy when our children were found.

It is an awesome thought that our dear heavenly Father feels pain, as only God can, over His lost children and oh, there are so many of them! And yes, He experiences such joy, as only God can, when one lost child is found.

In the Gospel of Luke (chapter 15) Jesus tells three stories about losing and finding. He talks about a lost sheep, a lost coin and a lost boy. Each story demonstrates the loser's sense of loss and then the thrill of rediscovery. Jesus is trying to get us to understand what it feels like to be God. In his book *What's So Amazing About Grace* (Zondervan, 1997), Philip Yancey imagines God saying, 'When one of those two-legged humans pays attention to Me it feels like I just reclaimed My most valuable possession which I had given up for lost.'

According to Jesus, there is a party in heaven when one lost child returns. And we need to realise that we are all lost children if we choose to follow our own wilful ways. But turn back to God and there is rejoicing in heaven over us. Isn't that amazing?

As Henri Nouwen put it, 'God rejoices. Not because the problems of the world have been solved, not because all human pain and suffering have come to an end, nor because thousands of people have been converted and are now praising Him for His good news. No, God rejoices because one of His children who was lost has been found' (*The Return Of The Prodigal Son: A Story Of Homecoming* (Darton, Longman & Todd Ltd, 1994).

To all His lost children – He is looking, He is waiting and He says, '*Please come home.*'

Dear heavenly Father, please help me to believe how precious I am to You. If I have been wandering, I choose to come back home to You. Please give me the grace to live a life of obedience under Your blessing. Amen.

46. *The performer in me*

According to my father, when I was two I scrambled onto the stage at the end of Redcar pier and sang 'Baa Baa Black Sheep' to a captive audience. Was I really *so* precocious?

Schooldays arrived, and at home we were encouraged to recite our latest poem or sing a song from *The National Song Book*.

Even after the arrival of our first wireless set we still made our own entertainment and as the eldest of the family I thoroughly enjoyed organising 'concerts' for our parents. We had a dressing-up box, and by far the most glamorous thing in it was a long, green satin 1920s dress. We vied with each other for the role that would entitle us to wear it. I probably used my senior status in order to hog the role *and* the dress. How I preened myself as I sat enfolded in its shimmering glory! Was I really *so* obnoxious?

In 1938 we spent two weeks by the sea at Redcar. For me, the highlight of the holiday was the twice daily beach show; every performance the same yet I never missed *one*! Their opening number 'The Optimists of 1938' was heaven to my young ears; how ironic in the light of the events of the next few years. However, August 1938 saw me hanging over the sea wall waiting for every show and wishing that I could be up there performing.

With the war came evacuation. Together with three other girls, I was billeted with a titled lady and thus thrown into a different world, a new world of wealth and culture. Not in the

least daunted, I organised concerts for *her* entertainment!
I wonder what she thought about us? I will never know, but
I thought we were good – after all, I'd learnt my skills at the
Redcar beach show!

It is quite amusing to look back on those innocent childhood
days of performing but there is nothing amusing in the
realisation that I was often performing in later life, by trying
to be what I was not. You may well wonder why I would do that.
Isn't it a human tendency to want to impress people, please
people, live up to others' expectations of us? I believe it is.
Praise is music to our ears.

The Bible tells us that many of the Jewish leaders denied
Jesus because they loved the praise of men rather than the
praise of God (John 12:42–43).

Jesus Himself lived and died to do His Father's will. He did
not seek praise from man. How can you and I be God pleasers?
Jesus says, "'… The Lord our God is the one and only God.
And you must love him with all your heart and soul and mind
and strength." The second is: "You must love others as much
as yourself." No other commandments are greater than these'
(Mark 12:29–31).

Surely a lifetime's work, but as we try to do everything for our
audience of one He, by His Holy Spirit, will empower us.

*Purify our hearts, Lord, that we may be changed from
one degree of glory to the next. Amen.*

47. *What does he do?*

One day, some years ago, I received phone calls from two of my sons. It was just before Christmas and they had both been to see their young daughters' schools' Nativity plays. 'How lovely,' I enthused to John, 'and what was Lucy?' 'Lucy was a cow,' replied John, with fatherly pride. 'She had to "moo" twice.' My grandmotherly heart was affronted! How could such a lowly role have been given to my bright young granddaughter?

On to the second phone call – 'and what was Hannah?' I asked Richard, with some trepidation. 'Hannah was an angel,' came the reply. My heart glowed! 'In fact she was the *chief* angel,' said Richard. I burst with pride and felt certain Hannah must have a good teacher!

Well, both my reactions were wrong, and I see that they were both rooted in pride. The world's influence seeps so insidiously into our thoughts that we can easily go with the flow and judge people by the jobs they do or their positions in society.

People's positions in life are usually the result of their background and upbringing; some have been privileged, others severely underprivileged.

And then there are people who deliberately elect to surrender their privileges and live alongside the outcasts of society. I am greatly challenged by the young Christians I know who are doing this, and I recognise they are following in the footsteps of their master, Jesus.

How sobering to read in the Gospel of Mark: people said Jesus was no better than them because 'he's just a carpenter ...' (Mark 6:3). They looked at His job and not at Him!

In his book, *3:16 – The Numbers Of Hope* (Thomas Nelson Inc., 2007) Max Lucado reminds us that when Joseph and Mary celebrated Jesus' birth, their temple offering was two turtledoves; the gift of the poor. From that we can assume they would have lived in the poorest part of the town. He goes on to say that Jesus would have dirty hands, sweat-stained shirts and, according to Isaiah, 'In God's eyes he was like a tender green shoot, sprouting from a root in dry and sterile ground. But in our eyes there was no attractiveness at all, nothing to make us want him' (Isaiah 53:2).

Why did Jesus come down from heaven and endure all that? So that we can know that He knows how we feel.

PS. Years later when I talked to Lucy about being a cow in the play, she said, 'I was a very good cow.' Out of the mouths of babes?

Dear Lord, please help me to look beyond someone's job to the person doing it and to be willing to give my time, a listening ear and a caring heart. Amen.

48. *Thoughts on a Christmas stocking!*

I vividly remember the intense excitement of Christmas Eve when I was a child. Nothing can compare with it; the mystery, the anticipation, the fear in case 'he' didn't come – they all combined to make this the most special of nights.

We hung up our stockings, names attached, and shouted up the chimney, trying to sound not *too* greedy and remembering to be polite, then up to bed for the long night!

Father Christmas was faithful; he always came. Our presents were very simple but they delighted us. Except … except for the year when I was about six. I crept downstairs at the crack of dawn, opened the door, and with *huge* relief saw that he'd been. My delight knew no bounds at the sight of the baby doll peeping out of the top of the stocking. Hugging her, I ran upstairs to show my parents what Santa had brought me. They then had the unenviable task of telling me I'd got the wrong stocking; the baby doll was for my little sister! I was then persuaded to search in my own stocking and there I found *my* doll, a four-inch china doll, jointed, pretty, and wearing a blue dress. The sad thing was that I had fallen in love with the baby doll which I could cuddle and this pretty little thing which I could only look at; well, she never won my affection.

G.K. Chesterton had a childlike delight in everyday things. Referring to children's delight in what they take out of their stockings on Christmas mornings, he suggested that what we put *into* our stockings each day – that is, our legs – are a much greater cause for gratitude. In Psalm 139 the psalmist proclaimed, 'I praise you because I am fearfully and wonderfully made; your works are wonderful, I know that full well' (Psalm 139:14). That baby doll and the china doll are long since gone but all these years on and my legs are still working! Quite wonderful! It's all too easy to take for granted the way God has made us and kept us.

A visiting preacher at my church spoke of a sobering lesson he'd had when working in a large store. At the end of a hard day he was irritated to be called to a checkout to sort out a problem. A customer had been asked to sign the back of his cheque and had requested a chair before doing so. Exasperated, our man went in search of one. Imagine his feelings when he returned with the chair for the customer who then sat down and signed the cheque with his foot – he had no hand!

Dear God, please forgive me for my ingratitude. Thank You for creating me. Thank You for keeping me. And thank You that I now know and have received Your greatest gift – Jesus. Amen.

49. *What if?*

One thing we all have in common is that we all have ancestors – parents, grandparents, great-grandparents and so on, back through the generations.

Try to imagine how our ancestors would have responded had someone suggested that one day men would fly in machines over oceans and mountains and would even walk on the moon? These ideas would have seemed unimaginable and yet we now know that they were not unattainable dreams.

Perhaps it's because man has achieved so much that many in this day and age find it hard to accept that there is someone greater and cleverer than the most powerful, intelligent human being; someone who has given mankind the promise of life after death.

But – *what if* the Bible is true? *What if* there is an all-knowing, all-powerful God who loves us and longs for us to return to Him as Father? *What if* Jesus, His Son, did leave heaven and come to earth to die on the cross, taking the punishment we deserve upon Himself, so as to make us fit for heaven? *What if* Jesus did rise from the dead, thus defeating death? *What if* He really has prepared a heavenly home for all who will accept Him as their Saviour and Lord? Do these seem ridiculous suggestions? But just *what if* they're true? Should we explore thme or ignore them?

In his book *The Reason Why*, Robert Laidlaw tells of two friends who went to law school. One became a judge but the other wasted his life, broke the law and finished up in court.

Sitting in the judge's seat was his old friend! Everyone wondered what kind of sentence he would pass. To their surprise he demanded the full penalty of the law. Then came a bigger surprise. The judge stepped down from his seat and said, 'Not only have I passed sentence upon him, but I will stand chargeable with his debts.' In that moment the judge became the redeemer.

Like the man in the dock, we've all been guilty of breaking God's laws. Jesus came down from His *heavenly* seat, put on the garment of humanity and endured the punishment we all deserve.

God gives each one of us the freedom to choose. We can accept or reject His gift of salvation. Perhaps you have never thought about these truths before, or perhaps you've thought about them and didn't know what to do. If the prayer below sums up how you feel and what you wish to do, then pray it sincerely and God *will* welcome you as His child because you will have put your faith in the finished work of Jesus on the cross.

Lord God, I've been wrong. I now see that You sent Jesus to die on the cross for my sins. Lord, I want to repent and believe in Jesus and what He did for me. Please forgive me for the way I have treated You and those around me and for the wrong things I have thought and done. Please come and take charge of my life, and be my Lord and friend. I ask this in the name of Jesus. Amen.

50. *The gift of forgiveness*

Nelson Mandela went to prison longing for freedom for his own people. They were the oppressed of the land and he had good cause to hate the white people who imprisoned him for twenty-seven years.

Yet, while in prison, a strange thing happened in his heart. He changed from desiring freedom for his own people to desiring freedom for *all* people – black *and* white, the oppressor *and* the oppressed. I would say that though he was still behind bars he had become a free man. The experience of receiving God's forgiveness is described very dramatically in one of Charles Wesley's great hymns:

> *Long my imprisoned spirit lay*
> *Fast bound in sin and nature's night;*
> *Thine eye diffused a quickening ray –*
> *I woke, the dungeon flamed with light;*
> *My chains fell off, my heart was free;*
> *I rose, went forth and followed Thee.*

Forgiveness is a gift from God. It is God we offend when we sin, so He is the One to whom we must go to confess our sins and to receive forgiveness. Our proud hearts may find this a hard thing to do but it is the only way. We can be sure God is waiting for us, full of grace and mercy. He longs to see our chains fall off as we receive forgiveness. The apostle Paul wrote,

'So there is now no condemnation awaiting those who belong to Christ Jesus. For the power of the life-giving Spirit – and this power is mine through Christ Jesus – has freed me from the vicious circle of sin and death' (Romans 8:1–2). Once we realise our continuous need of God's merciful forgiveness, it should cause us to be merciful and forgiving towards others. There is a challenging verse in the Lord's Prayer: 'Forgive us our trespasses as we forgive those who trespass against us.' It's a beautiful truth that we can give the gift of forgiveness to those who have hurt us.

Lack of forgiveness can be at the root of physical illnesses. I heard this story from a young missionary home on leave from Burundi. He showed us a picture of himself holding a little African child who looked about three: in fact he was eight. The child's parents had been hacked to death before his eyes when he *was* three and he literally stopped growing. Tender love and care were lavished upon him but to no avail.

However, shortly before our missionary friend came to England on leave, amazing things were happening in the little boy's life. He had been taught about Jesus and had been able to forgive the murderers. What a miracle of grace! And the next miracle was that he began to grow! I am reminded of the words of Jesus: 'Unless you turn to God from your sins and become as little children, you will never get into the kingdom of Heaven' (Matthew 18:2).

Dear Lord, please help me to keep short accounts with You, confessing my sins and believing that I am forgiven. Thank You for Your amazing grace. Please help me to be like You in giving the gift of forgiveness to others. Amen.

51. *The most important date*

It is a sad fact of life that we often unwittingly let people down. And equally, we ourselves can frequently be let down.

I attended a church school and each year excitement rose as the time for the Christmas bazaar approached. The school hall was transformed into a market-place; stalls, games with prizes, all the fun of the fair – and with an invited VIP for the official opening!

One day, when I was five, I was given an envelope to take home. Little did I know that it contained news of the utmost importance in our little world! *I* had been chosen to present a bouquet to the important lady opening the bazaar that year.

Rehearsals began. The headmistress would take me to the school hall and onto the stage. Then, she and I would rehearse the ritual. As the speech finished I was to walk onto the stage, curtsey to the lady, present her with the bouquet, curtsey again and withdraw. It had to be perfect!

At home, preparations of a different kind were going on. An aunt made my dress, long and apple-green in colour. I thought it was beautiful. Lacy mitts and dainty slippers were dyed to match, and diamantés from my mother's wedding shoes were sewn onto the slippers. Nothing was overlooked for this most important of dates.

The big day came. Dressed in my finery and carrying a

beautiful, trailing bouquet of pink roses, I was guardedly escorted to the wings of the stage, waiting until the big moment came. However, unknown to me, the important lady hadn't arrived and an elderly priest was doing the honours in her place. At the end of his speech I walked on to the stage, curtseyed and presented him with the bouquet. In his awkwardness perhaps, he made a joke of the situation, because I was conscious of laughter going through the hall. It was my turn to feel embarrassed as I made my final curtsey and retreated. What an anticlimax!

Perhaps that was the first time I was conscious of feeling foolish. How wonderful to know that there is someone who will never let us down. The apostle Paul was totally convinced of that. In his second letter to the young Timothy, he says, 'I won't be around to help you very much longer. My time has almost run out. Very soon now I will be on my way to heaven. I have fought long and hard for my Lord, and through it all I have kept true to him … In heaven a crown is waiting for me which the Lord, the righteous Judge, will give me on that great day of his return. And not just to me, but to all those whose lives show that they are eagerly looking forward to his coming back again' (2 Timothy 4:6–8).

Now, that is a date which I do not want to miss and I know Jesus will not let me down.

Help me, Lord, to run the race with perseverance.
Thank You for Your promise of a crown of glory.
Marantha. Come, Lord Jesus, come.

52. *There will be a crown of glory*

There were many celebrations to mark the new millennium, and for me one of the highlights was a parade of past and present Wimbledon stars. Every player who qualified for the honour was presented with an engraved crystal plate, whilst the commentator gave a scintillating account of their achievements over film footage of their peak performances. Exciting, yet at the same time very moving because the oldest was in a wheelchair, and another limped bravely along the length of the red carpet with the aid of a walking stick. Many could scarcely be identified as the sparkling athletes they once were, a glimpse of whose past glories we'd just seen. I recall wondering whether that moment of honour and glory was perhaps tinged with sadness as we saw the evidence of their ageing and mortality.

Death will come to us all, and we know not the day, nor the hour. Our tendency is to choose to put this unpalatable fact onto the backburner of our lives!

Shatteringly, on Christmas morning 2007, my family and I were brought face to face with the harsh reality of death when my son Paul, aged just forty-two, died very suddenly. Paul was my youngest child and the brother of Miriam, John and Richard. Not only were *we* shocked, but so too were the hospital staff. Our hearts were broken and sadness overwhelmed us. For me this was the hardest loss. Only those who have lost a child will understand. Yet we realised that we were being upheld by the prayers of God's people as we sensed His presence and His peace. We experienced the reality of Psalm 23 which says, 'Yea, though I walk through the valley of the shadow of death, I will fear no evil: for thou art with me …' (Psalm 23:4, AV). He was with us and He *is* with us. And most precious of all, we have the assurance that Paul is at peace in the presence of our faithful God.

As a family we received the strength to press on and miraculously I was able to complete this book. The apostle Paul wrote, 'I strain to reach the end of the race and receive the prize for which God is calling us up to heaven because of what Christ Jesus did for us' (Philippians 3:14).

Thank God that death is not the end, but the gateway to fullness of life through Jesus who is the Way.

> *And I … saw the Holy City, the new Jerusalem, coming down from God out of heaven …*
> *I heard a loud shout from the throne, saying, 'Look, the home of God is now among men … He will wipe away all tears from their eyes, and there shall be no more death, or sorrow, or crying, or pain. All of that has gone forever.'*
> *And the one sitting on the throne said, 'See, I am making all things new!'*
>
> *Revelation 21:2–5*

The flame of love

All in Your hands, sweet Saviour,
All in Your hands I place
The gladness and the sadness
'Neath the fountain of Your grace.

I see Your heart on fire, O Lord,
On fire with love for me.
I place my heart within that heart
O listen to my plea.

Please let my heart be set on fire
And may that flame burn bright,
That lonely souls will feel Your love
And lives be set aright.

Please take me, take me as I am
And change this heart of stone,
That all my days I'll sing Your praise
And worship You alone.

National Distributors

UK: (and countries not listed below)
CWR, Waverley Abbey House, Waverley Lane, Farnham, Surrey GU9 8EP.
Tel: (01252) 784700 Outside UK (44) 1252 784700 Email: mail@cwr.org.uk

AUSTRALIA: KI Entertainment, Unit 21 317-321 Woodpark Road, Smithfield, New South Wales 2164.
Tel: 1 0800 850 777 Fax: 02 9604 3699 Email:sales@kientertainment.com.au

CANADA: David C Cook Distribution Canada, PO Box 98, 55 Woodslee Avenue, Paris, Ontario N3L 3E5.
Tel: 1800 263 2664 Email: swansons@cook.ca

GHANA: Challenge Enterprises of Ghana, PO Box 5723, Accra.
Tel: (021) 222437/223249 Fax: (021) 226227 Email: ceg@africaonline.com.gh

HONG KONG: Cross Communications Ltd, 1/F, 562A Nathan Road, Kowloon.
Tel: 2780 1188 Fax: 2770 6229 Email: cross@crosshk.com

INDIA: Crystal Communications, 10-3-18/4/1, East Marredpalli, Secunderabad – 500026, Andhra Pradesh.
Tel/Fax: (040) 27737145 Email: crystal_edwj@rediffmail.com

KENYA: Keswick Books and Gifts Ltd, PO Box 10242, Nairobi.
Tel: (02) 331692/226047 Fax: (02) 728557 Email: keswick@swiftkenya.com

MALAYSIA: Salvation Book Centre (M) Sdn Bhd, 23 Jalan SS 2/64, 47300 Petaling Jaya, Selangor.
Tel: (03) 78766411/78766797 Fax: (03) 78757066/78756360 Email: info@salvationbookcentre.com
Canaanland, No. 25 Jalan PJU 1A/41B, NZX Commercial Centre, Ara Jaya, 47301 Petaling Jaya, Selangor.
Tel: (03) 7885 0540/1/2 Fax: (03) 7885 0545 Email: info@canaanland.com.my

NEW ZEALAND: KI Entertainment, Unit 21 317-321 Woodpark Road, Smithfield, New South Wales 2164,
Australia. Tel: 0 800 850 777 Fax: 02 9604 3699 Email: sales@kientertainment.com.au

NIGERIA: FBFM, Helen Baugh House, 96 St Finbarr's College Road, Akoka, Lagos.
Tel: (01) 7747429/4700218/825775/827264 Email: fbfm@hyperia.com

PHILIPPINES: OMF Literature Inc, 776 Boni Avenue, Mandaluyong City.
Tel: (02) 531 2183 Fax: (02) 531 1960 Email: gloadlaon@omflit.com

SINGAPORE: Alby Commercial Enterprises Pte Ltd, 95 Kallang Avenue #04-00,
AIS Industrial Building, 339420. Tel: (65) 629 27238 Fax: (65) 629 27235 Email: marketing@alby.com.sg

SOUTH AFRICA: Struik Christian Books, 80 MacKenzie Street, PO Box 1144, Cape Town 8000.
Tel: (021) 462 4360 Fax: (021) 461 3612 Email: info@struikchristianmedia.co.za

SRI LANKA: Christombu Publications (Pvt) Ltd, Bartleet House, 65 Braybrooke Place, Colombo 2.
Tel: (9411) 2421073/2447665 Email: dhanad@bartleet.com

USA: David C Cook Distribution Canada, PO Box 98, 55 Woodslee Avenue, Paris, Ontario N3L 3E5, Canada.
Tel: 1800 263 2664 Email: swansons@cook.ca

For email addresses, visit the CWR website: www.cwr.org.uk
CWR is a Registered Charity – Number 294387
CWR is a Limited Company registered in England – Registration Number 1990308

Day and Residential Courses
Counselling Training
Leadership Development
Biblical Study Courses
Regional Seminars
Ministry to Women
Daily Devotionals
Books and DVDs
Conference Centre

Trusted all Over the World

CWR HAS GAINED A WORLDWIDE reputation as a centre of excellence for Bible-based training and resources. From our headquarters at Waverley Abbey House, Farnham, England, we have been serving God's people for over 40 years with a vision to help apply God's Word to everyday life and relationships. The daily devotional *Every Day with Jesus* is read by nearly a million readers an issue in more than 150 countries, and our unique courses in biblical studies and pastoral care are respected all over the world. Waverley Abbey House provides a conference centre in a unique setting.

For free brochures on our seminars and courses, conference facilities, or a catalogue of CWR resources, please contact us at the following address:
CWR, Waverley Abbey House, Waverley Lane, Farnham, Surrey GU9 8EP, UK

Telephone: +44 (0)1252 784700
Email: mail@cwr.org.uk
Website: www.cwr.org.uk

CWR Applying God's Word
to everyday life and relationships

Our pocket devotionals make ideal gifts

Inspiring daily devotions by Selwyn Hughes for every day of the year, selected from *Every Day with Jesus.*

- Life's Hidden Agendas
- Things Most Surely Believed
- Building a More Effective Prayer Life
- The Power of a New Perspective
- Being Alert to Spiritual Danger
- Riding the Winds of Adversity

ISBN: 978-1-85345-464-6

- The Vision of God
- The Marks of a Christian Church
- Come, Holy Spirit
- When Sovereignty Surprises
- The Stone of Stumbling
- More than Conquerors

ISBN: 978-1-85345-465-3

£7.99 each

Refresh your soul and strengthen your faith

Our *Every Day with Jesus* Spoken Word CDs feature meditations and music blended together for a powerful devotional experience.

£9.99 each

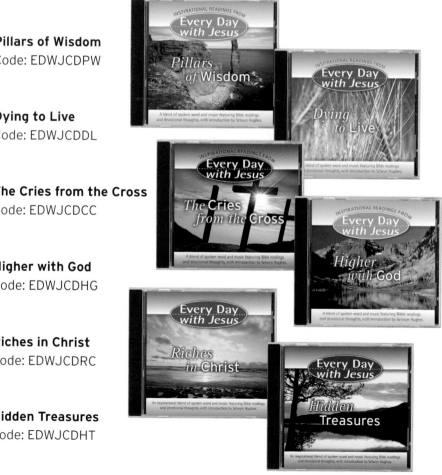

Pillars of Wisdom
Code: EDWJCDPW

Dying to Live
Code: EDWJCDDL

The Cries from the Cross
Code: EDWJCDCC

Higher with God
Code: EDWJCDHG

Riches in Christ
Code: EDWJCDRC

Hidden Treasures
Code: EDWJCDHT

Special gifts for yourself or others

These elegant books have white, bonded-leather covers with silver foil lettering, silver-edged pages and each comes with a protective slipcase and ribbon marker.

Perfect for baptisms, christenings, first communions, anniversaries and landmark birthdays, this full-colour gift book will encourage and inspire through Bible verses, poems, hymns, thoughts and prayers.

Special to God by Catherine Butcher
108-pages, 108x152mm,
ISBN: 978-1-85345-365-6
Only £9.99

Invite your loving Father into every twist and turn of your life with this collection of original prayers for the relationships, storms and celebrations of life – and much more.

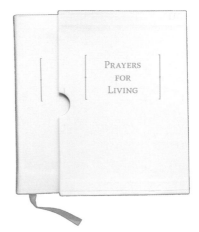

Prayers for Living by Wendy Bray
112 full-colour pages, 108x152mm,
ISBN: 978-1-85345-496-7
Only £9.99

Prices correct at time of printing and exclusive of p&p